THE THEATRE IN POLAND

Roman Szydłowski

THE THEATRE
IN POLAND

INTERPRESS PUBLISHERS, WARSAW 1972

Graphic layout:
JERZY KĘPKIEWICZ

Translator:
CHRISTINA CENKALSKA

Polish Editor:
ELŻBIETA MULICKA

Technical Editor:
GRZEGORZ BIELAWSKI

Photographs by:
M. CZUDOWSKI, J. GRELOWSKI, B. ŁOPIEŃSKI, J. MOREK,
F. MYSZKOWSKI, T. JANKOWSKI, J. GARDZIELEWSKA,
W. PLEWIŃSKI, E. HARTWIG, CZ. KUCHTA, Z. ŁAGOCKI, Z. ŁUBAK,
Z. MATUSZEWSKI and S. WYSZOMIRSKA

This is the one thousand two hundred and fifty-eighth publication of
Interpress Publishers

PRINTED IN POLAND

This book appears also in French, German, Polish, Russian and Spanish.

PRASOWE ZAKŁADY GRAFICZNE RSW „PRASA" — BYDGOSZCZ

LIST OF CONTENTS

CHAPTER I

THE STYLE OF THE POLISH THEATRE

A theatre's rank and significance are primarily determined by its style. Style is developed over a long period of years and is the result of creative experiment by brilliant personalities of the theatre. Style reflects the spirit of a people and its specific traits. These in turn are mirrored in literature and art. The more original and the richer the style of a theatre, the more inimitable features it possesses, and the more it has to say both in substance and form the greater its significance and impact on public and national life. The Polish theatre is highly individualized, rich and unique. Its image is marked by the following four main features: 1) involvement in the affairs of the country and the people, 2) poetic character, 3) painterly vision of the world, 4) ironic and satirical view, a sense of humour and a love of the grotesque and exaggeration and a preference for a clear construction outline.

The Polish theatre concerned itself with problems most vital to the destiny of the nation practically from the beginning of its existence. So it was at the close of the 16th century (hence two centuries before the decline of the Poland of the gentry) when Jan Kochanowski warned the nation against imminent catastrophe "O unruly kingdom standing on the verge of disaster." So it was at the close of the 18th century when Franciszek Zabłocki branded the corruption and demoralization of the gentry in *Fircyk w zalotach* (A Dandy Goes Acourting) and when Julian Ursyn Niemcewicz came out in support of the reform programme put forth by the Four Year Sejm (Parliament) and the May 3rd Constitution in his *Powrót posła* (Return of the Deputy). Wojciech Bogusławski, called the father of the national theatre, treated the stage as a school for national education. His song-play *Krakowiacy i górale* (The Cracovians and the Mountaineers), some of the couplets were composed on the day of the opening, sounded the battle cry to the Kościuszko Insurrection of 1794. Ardent words echoed from the Polish stage at all times, rallying the people to battle in the years of bondage and summoning them to put their efforts to constructive work in years when the first and foremost task was to restore and to rebuild the liberated country. In the years of partition, the Polish language was banished from the schools, offices and even from the streets. The theatre was the only place where the people could listen to their beloved language and learn about civic duties in the small and important affairs of their country. The Polish theatre sought to speak of the major issues of the country and to brand the flaws and defects of national character. It was concerned with giving the people an education in patriotism. Involved, political, philosophical and critical of national shortcomings, the Polish theatre felt a natural kinship with the dramas of Shakespeare and Schiller, Calderon and Lope de Vega and with the philosophical comedies of Molière as well as with Corneille's fervently patriotic *Le Cid* and *Mariage de Figaro* by Beaumarchais.

The patriotism and involvement in national affairs was synchronized with poetry and metaphor in the Polish theatre. The Polish drama and the Polish theatre was poetic at the time of Rej and Kochanowski and has remained poetic to this day. Consequently, it is not a coincidence that the finest Polish stage works are written by poets. The Polish theatre evinced little enthusiasm for narrow realism and domestic drama. It is true that the great period of naturalism in Europe of the turn of the century left its mark in Poland as well. Reflective of the trend were the works of such distinguished Polish authors as Gabriela Zapolska, Tadeusz Rittner and Włodzimierz Perzyński. But the period also produced such artists as Wyspiański and his poetic theatre. The dramatic style and ideas of an epic theatre it represented projected its image far into the 20th century.

Poetry found its artistic counterpart in stage design and costumes. The art of poetry is the ability to express thought in concise and beautiful terms. The art of the painter is the ability to think in pictures. The two compose a pair and are united in the Polish dramas. The greatest Polish poets of the theatre thought in pictures and the Polish theatre which interprets their works today has learned to think in pictures. That is why stage design is so important a feature of the Polish theatre.

In Poland, stage designers not only design sets, or the functional acting area, and the costumes, but also take part in the production and the staging of the plays.

There are few countries in the world where theatres work in such close collaboration with plastic artists as in Poland. There are not many countries where one sees so much colour on stage and where the sets are applauded when the curtain goes up and before the action starts. Finally, there are not many countries where stage designers turn stage directors (witness

Józef Szajna) and where the most distinguished directors are graduates of Art Academies (Konrad Swinarski and Andrzej Wajda). The last two directors design sets to many of the plays they direct and work closely with stage designers, thus putting their early training to use.

Many of the most creative ideas on staging have come out from discussions between stage director and stage designer. Neither the first nor the second works in isolation. The final stage design is often developed in the course of rehearsals. The stage designer is a member of the company, permanently employed by the theatre. Noted stage designers have worked with the same directors for years. In that time they come to know the director's style and artistic preferences; they establish a common language and become partners and collaborators in the staging of plays.

Irony holds a special position in the Polish theatre. The ironic point of view serves to unmask and castigate flaws and frailties while distortion and grotesque, by virtue of their disparity with a naturalistic photograph of reality, communicate a deep and complete truth about life. The use of the parenthesis in painting is the same in poetry, that is to isolate a problem and to emphasize it by taking a long view of it and to clarify the meaning of a thing by looking at it from distance. A sense of humour has been a significant Polish national trait for centuries. It saved the Poles from a number of disasters and helped them survive the darkest years of foreign bondage, war and occupation. It would be odd indeed if satire were not present in the Polish theatre.

We discover it in the 16th century dramatic works of Mikołaj Rej of Nagłowice; the ironic stanzas in *Dzia-*

dy (Forefathers' Eve) have lost none of their bite even today. We also discover remarkable examples of satirical stage verse in the works of the Romantic poets of the 19th century Słowacki and Norwid. Wyspiański's *Wesele* (The Wedding) and *Wyzwolenie* (Liberation) are national tragi-comedies of the finest quality. The line of evolution leads directly from these two plays to the tragi-farces of Stanisław Ignacy Witkiewicz: *Matka* (Mother), *Oni* (They), *Gyubal Wahazar* and *Szewcy* (The Cobblers). Though the plays may strike one at first as absurd, yet the view they take of Poland and the world is prophetic. The author has sounded a warning of the dire peril threatening modern humanity, disclosing and branding this danger. The mordant irony we find in the plays of Witold Gombrowicz, Sławomir Mrożek, Tadeusz Różewicz and other poets of the youngest generation of dramatists writing in Poland today.

Laughter is healing, laughter disarms the enemy, laughter may also hurt at times. The Polish theatre never rejected or feared laughter. It cannot tolerate vacant laughter. Attempts to suppress satire and laughter was made by those to whom it was more deadly than the sharp thrust of a blade or the slash of a broadsword. Bishop Ignacy Krasicki, 18th century author of what are the most remarkable aphorisms and satire in the Polish language, said at one time: "True virtue does not fear criticism."

What then does the style of the Polish theatre consist of? Taking shape over the centuries, its origins can be traced from the plebeian spectacles, mystery plays, peasant puppet theatres carried through the villages and hamlets at Christmas time, through the nativity plays and religious emotions generated by Christmas carols and to the sleigh rides and palace balls, the soaring inspiration of Romantic and neo-romantic poetry and finally to the modern stage plays. The style is represented today by a synthesis of the poetic and the political theatre. The style of the modern theatre is widely diversified. It covers both the grand stage spectaculars, vibrant with light and colour, the richly resplendent monumental theatre — a synthesis of text, movement, pictorial scenes, music and pantomime as well as the nearly ascetic stage productions. The Pantomime Theatre (whose principal feature is directed movement) and the experiments of the Grotowski Laboratory Theatre, where the actor's body is the very material and substance of the theatre, also make a contribution to the modern theatre.

CHAPTER II

HISTORICAL OUTLINE

The contemporary Polish theatre may therefore be said to possess a distinct image and an original style. How did this come about? What elements combined to create this style? How did it evolve?

In order to answer these questions, we must go back to the beginning. The Polish theatre is one of the oldest in the world. Its beginnings go back to the Middle Ages. The first plays were religious and sacral in character. The earliest play to come down to our times was called *Officium Sepulchri;* it is dated somewhere in the end of the 12th and the beginning of the 13th century. The play is found in the collection of the Cracow chapter house. Also extant are over a dozen other Latin church dialogues between Mary, the angels and the apostles at the sepulchre of the Christ. In the beginning, the dialogues were recited inside the church in front of the altar, later the action was moved outside the church gates, then to the cemeteries and finally to the town squares and streets. The early liturgical and religious dialogues were later embellished with a growing number of secular elements. Deacons, clerics, students and members of craft guilds performed in these plays. Though it is certain that the Latin texts were replaced by Polish dialogues in the 15th century, the assumption is that Latin was already phased out at the close of the 14th century.

The earliest Easter play to come down to our day is *Historya o Chwalebnym Zmartwychwstaniu Pańskim* (The History of the Lord's Glorious Resurrection). Taken down by Mikołaj of Wilkowiecko, a Częstochowa monk, in the 16th century, it contains parts of the earlier text from the 15th and even the 14th century. *The History of the Lord's Glorious Resurrection* received its first production in modern times in 1923 by Leon Schiller. Kazimierz Dejmek's adaptation came in 1961.

The 16th century witnessed the flowering of Polish culture. The power of the Polish state and its thriving economy were conducive to the development of literature and other branches of art. Tolerance and freedom of thought were propitious to unhampered discussion in which reform and modern moral concepts constituted the main interest. At the time, Polish humanists maintained lively contacts with centres of European thought. The University of Cracow (now the Jagiellonian), founded in 1364, had already produced a number of intellectuals who held their own with the most learned and cultivated minds of the age. Poles continued their education in Padua and Paris, they travelled to Basel and to Amsterdam and attended Italian and French universities and German, Dutch and Swiss schools. Nicolaus Copernicus made his momentous discovery in distant Frombork, Paweł Włodkowic (Paulus Vladimiri), rector of the University of Cracow, astonished members of the Council of Constance with his farsighted views on the laws of nations, Hieronimus Łaski remained in close contact with Erasmus of Rotterdam and bought his library, Jan Kochanowski read with avid interest not only Dante and Petrarch but also the seven contemporary poets, who went by the appellation Pléiade as well as du Bellay and Ronsard whom he met during one of his stays in Paris.

The Reformation soon took its place in the Polish drama next to the Catholic theme. The most distinguished representative of the new trend was Mikołaj Rej, author of *Żywot Józefa* (The Life of Joseph) and *Rozmowy między panem, wójtem i plebanem* (Dialogues Between the Lord, Bailiff and Parish Priest) and many other clearly didactic works.

The subject of politics appeared on the stage in 1578 with Jan Kochanowski's poetic play *Odprawa posłów greckich* (The Dismissal of the Greek Envoys). Though the action was set in the times of the Trojan war, yet in substance the author sounded a warning that was aimed at contemporary public opinion, for threatening clouds were already gathering on the horizons of Poland's political life.

English actors came to Poland in the early part of the 17th century. They appeared in Shakespeare's plays in the town of Elbląg during the lifetime of the Bard and visited Warsaw in 1611 and then again in 1616. King Władysław IV was a great admirer of the opera. He had one of the chambers of the Warsaw castle adapted to the needs of the theatre in the 17th century. His brother and successor, John II Casimir, had a greater interest in the dramatic theatre. John II had close French connections; he spent many years of his stormy life in France and married a French woman. He attached greater significance to the political role of the theatre. It was under his reign (in 1662) that the first Polish performance of Corneille's *Le Cid* was given in a beautiful translation by Andrzej Morsztyn. The example set by the royal court was followed by Polish magnates. They established theatres in their residences and either diverted themselves by taking part in the plays or invited foreign troupes and actors to instruct serfs who betrayed a talent for the theatre.

The plebeian theatre developed in Poland in the 16th and 17th century as well. Actors of the *commedia dell' arte* adapted to Polish needs appeared in town streets and squares. Many of them were students of the University of Cracow, strolling players, who earned their living in this fashion. Working in the summer months they could then study in the winter free of care. The Rybałt comedy (a name popularized by K. Badecki referring to anonymous, though not always, dramatic works, these being mostly satires that come closest to the harlequinades) that is most outstanding in its class is Piotr Baryka's *Z chłopa król* (The Peasant a King). At this time too *Tragedia o bogaczu i Łazarzu* (A Tragedy of a Rich Man and a Beggar) appeared in Gdańsk. At Pułtusk the Jesuits operated an interesting theatre whose aims were purely didactic. Similar aims underlay the activity of the Jesuit theatres connected with the schools operated by the order in Poland in the 16th and the 17th century.

The development of Polish culture was interrupted abruptly and tragically in the 17th century. There were three major causes for this: the economic and fiscal policies designed to protect the interests of the Polish gentry and the restricted rights of townsmen and peasants, the fierce campaign against the Reformation conducted by the Catholic church with the full support of the king, the magnates and a large part of the gentry and finally the Swedish invasion, war with the Cossacks and the dire effects of what is known in Polish history as the deluge which inundated the country in the middle of the 17th century.

At the close of the 17th century Poland was the picture of ruin and destitution. Foreign troops roamed the country, the towns were burned down, devastated and depopulated and to top it all the foreign Saxon dynasty evinced no interest in the reconstruction of the land. The motto "Eat and loosen your belt" reigned supreme under the Saxon king. Could the theatre thrive in these circumstances?

More than a hundred years elapsed before the people shook themselves free of the marasm and before the country raised itself out of ruin. Just when the situation grew more hopeful, the partition of Poland put an end to the independence of the country. The hundred years of continuous setbacks proved fatal. It was impossible to regain lost ground. The neighbouring countries, which had grown much faster in the meantime, had outdistanced Poland with regard to potential and organizational efficiency did not intend to tolerate a balance of power. Fortunately, work which was to bear throughout the 19th century and whose effects were to reach far into the 20th century was begun just before the zero hour struck. It was then that the theatre played its most distinguished and laudable role.

The last king of Poland Stanisław August Poniatowski was a highly educated and cultured man. He had travelled extensively as a young man, visiting Paris, Petersburg and London where he fell under the spell of Shakespeare. A year after he ascended to the throne of Poland, he founded a permanent Polish theatre open to the general public. The theatre inaugurated its activities on November 29th, 1765 with *Natręci* (The Intruders) by Józef Bielawski. At first foreign companies, such as the Italian opera, and French and German actors, appeared on the national Polish stage and for a time it seemed that the young and inexperienced Polish theatre would be dominated by foreign artists.

Soon, however, there emerged a man who made a major contribution to the triumph of the Polish repertory. He was Wojciech Bogusławski (1757—1829). True, his was a unique chance and he had a number of important advantages on his side. Being a member of the Polish gentry and an officer, he enjoyed a social privilege withheld from Polish actors, most of whom were either base born of former serfs acting in the theatres set up by Polish magnates. Bogusławski received his theatre training under the guidance of the Frenchman Louis Montbrun, a man of breeding who knew his trade well. He was a manager for a time of the newly established theatre. Bogusławski proved not only a talented actor and gifted stage director but also a highly imaginative dramatist, noted as well for his adroit stage adaptations of Polish and other literary works. He was also an energetic and efficient organizer of theatre life. He did not have an easy life at first. All manner of intrigues snatched from his grasp the objective he had staked out for himself, that is to establish high literary and artistic standards in the National Theatre of Warsaw. Fortunately, the king knew his own mind and proved a wise patron of the stage arts and friend of actors. Royal support tipped the scales in Bogusławski's favour.

A short dozen or so years before the downfall of the Polish Republic, a lasting foundation was laid for the theatre in Warsaw: a permanent professional stage with high artistic ambitions which presented Polish dramatic works and adaptations made expressly for the *Narodowy* (National) Theatre from world literature.

Not since the Renaissance, a period of dazzling splendour in 16th century Poland, was such lively intellectual activity noted in the country as toward the end of the 18th century. That was when Franciszek Zabłocki wrote his wise and witty comedies. Nor was he alone. There was a group of gifted comedy writers working in Poland then. Most notable among these were Franciszek Bohomolec and Julian Ursyn Niemcewicz. Next to *The Cracovians and the Mountaineers* and *Henryk IV na łowach* (Henry IV at the Chase), Bogusławski wrote plays that remain a part of the repertory of the Polish theatre to this day. He composed song-plays, that were distinctly Polish in character, and produced Polish versions of many works by Molière and other French dramatists. The action of the French plays was not only set in Poland but the characters were given Polish names and dressed in Polish costumes.

The vigorous development of the theatre was abruptly halted when, falling prey to the three powers — Austria, Prussia and Russia — Poland lost her independence in the final years of the 18th century. But even this national disaster failed to suppress intellectual activity and to destroy Polish culture. The theatre seized every opportunity to produce plays and to continue its activity against all odds. Bogusławski and his troupe toured the country, playing in the large and small Polish towns, establishing or stimulating the establishment of theatres in Cracow, Poznań, Kalisz and many other centres of the partitioned country.

Fate smiled at the Poles when the country was liberated and the Warsaw Duchy established in consequence of the Napoleonic war. This fact added fresh impetus to the Polish theatre. Even the sham of a Polish Kingdom ruled by the Russian tsar, that had been established by the decision of the Congress of Vienna, was enough to save the theatre. Cracow, proclaimed a free city by the victorious powers of occupation, took advantage of the situation with alacrity. Thus a second centre of Polish theatrical life was established. But Warsaw, being the wealthier of the two, attracted the best actors from the whole country. However, tsarist censorship was the more repressive. It became even more onerously restrictive after the collapse of the Polish November 1831 insurrection. In consequence of the disaster, the Polish Kingdom was dissolved and incorporated into the tsarist empire. Political and national repression increased in virulence in Warsaw after the fall of the January 1863 insurrection.

In 1848 Cracow was deprived of its freedom and incorporated into the Austrian Habsburg monarchy. In the first decades after the incorporation, efforts were made to Germanize the city and its population. Inevitably, this had a deleterious effect upon the position and activity of the Polish theatre there. The liberal policies introduced in all of Austria after 1866 also affected Galicia (as that part of Poland under Austrian dominion was called). National repression gave way to efforts to find a modus vivendi with the Polish population and principally with the Polish gentry and aristocracy.

It was then that leading Polish intellectuals and artists fled the Russian zone of occupation with its repression and deadening censorship. Notable among these was Stanisław Koźmian, noted authority on the theatre, who took over the management of the theatre of Cracow. On the other hand, prominent Cracow and Lvov actors tested their mettle in Warsaw. They were lured by the reputation attached to the "actor of the capital city" and by the high fees paid by the directors of government theatres. Thus, Helena Modrzejewska (Modjeska), greatest Polish actress of the 19th century, came to Warsaw where after a successful career in Cracow and Lvov (she scored her greatest triumphs in Shakespearean roles), she enthralled the Warsaw audiences. From Warsaw Modjeska went to America where her fame became worldwide. She was acclaimed the greatest Shakespearean actress even in the Bard's native land. The Polish actor Bogumił Dawison won notable success in the German theatre, specifically in the Burgtheater of Vienna.

It is clear from the above facts that the Polish theatre continued to flourish in the 19th century and that despite the many grave obstacles it encountered, it nevertheless established a reputation for high artistic standards. Polish drama fared much worse. The greatest Polish poets of the age lived in exile and wrote plays which they could not hope to see produced on any stage. The best dramatic work of Mickiewicz, *Forefathers' Eve* was not to be seen on the Polish stage until many decades after the author's death. Juliusz Słowacki and Cyprian Kamil Norwid wrote their dramas while living in exile. Zygmunt Krasiński wrote in the country but he dared not entertain the faintest hope that his plays would ever be produced. The only poet of note whose works were produced at the time of writing was Aleksander Fredro. His remarkable comedies are packed with profound observations of Polish life and scintillate with ribald old Polish humour and a sense of construction borrowed from the French. Fredro learned of French manners and philosophy during his stays in Paris and while serving in the Grand Army during the Napoleonic wars.

In the final analysis, the obstacles put in the way and bans on plays written by the Polish Romantic poets of the 19th century worked for the benefit of the Polish theatre. Mickiewicz and the other Romantic poets were free of the restrictions of aesthetic rules and the technical stage limitations of their time. The epic dramas they wrote were therefore a whole century ahead of their age. Notable efforts at production were made at the turn of this century followed by Leon Schiller's celebrated stage adaptations in the period between the two world wars after Poland's restoration in 1918. But not until the sixties and the seventies of the 20th century did the Polish theatre develop the techniques and the machinery which enabled it to give the best readings to date of these notable masterpieces. The process it not yet finished. Only artists richer by the experiences of Brecht and Artaud, Brooks and Strehler or Grotowski can do full justice to the plays.

No significant intellectual development or important art trend passed unnoticed in Poland. In the second half of the 19th century, the Cracow theatre was drawn into the sphere of influence of the German language countries. Poles quickly learned of the theatre reform and accomplishments of Duke von Meiningen, they were in constant touch with the Burgtheatre of Vienna's excellent acting school and maintained a lively interest in the work done by Brahm and Reinhardt. The then young Arnold Szyfman decided to introduce Reinhardt's theories in Poland.

The Polish theatre maintained an equally lively contact with the Russian theatre. Warsaw was then a part of the same country as Moscow and Petersburg.

From
Bernard Shaw

Phone & Wire: AYOT SAINT LAWRENCE.
CODICOTE 218. 12/7/1948 WELWYN, HERTS.

Dear Dr Szyfman
 On the 10th July bext I hope
you will remind your audience that
you wore the first to perform some
of my most famous plays.
 I think this places you as th
most farseeing manager in Europe
(including England), and the Teatr
Polski above London as a centre of
dramatic culture.

G.B.S.

A letter sent by G. B. Shaw to A. Szyfman on the 35th anniversary of the *Polski* Theatre in 1948

The best Russian theatres toured the land on the Vistula (the official designation for the part of Poland annexed by Russia). Stanislavsky and the Moscow Art Theatre visited Warsaw in 1905. The leading Polish stage critic of the period, Jan Lorentowicz, wrote an open letter to Stanislavsky explaining why the Polish public could not go to see the Moscow Art Theatre. Theatre artists did see the work of the then most interesting innovator and reformer of the theatre in Europe. Ludwik Solski, then director of the theatre of Cracow, set out for Warsaw from Cracow especially to see the Moscow Art Theatre.

Paris, the capital of the Polish émigrés over many long decades. It would have been hard to find a prominent Polish intellectual or artist who had not made a pilgrimage to Paris. Polish painters who had at first studied in Munich, now flocked to Paris. A trip to France was an indispensable part of the education of every Polish intellectual. Gabriela Zapolska, who in her later life wrote a number of excellent naturalistic plays, visited Paris and even appeared in André Antoine's *La Theátre Libre*. The young Polish doctor Tadeusz Żeleński, who arrived in Paris in order to complete his medical education, fell in love with the city. In the end he betrayed his chosen profession for the cabaret and songs, preferring the *Chat noir* to the dissecting room. Upon his return to Cracow, he and a group of his friends set up the *Zielony Balonik* (Green Balloon) cabaret. In the years between the two world wars he was to become Poland's leading drama critic and remarkable translator of French literature. Stanisław Wyspiański, the greatest Polish dramatist of the turn of the century, also knew Paris as did Tadeusz Rittner, son of an Austrian minister who made his home in Vienna and wrote both in Polish and German. His plays were performed on the Polish stage as well as in Vienna. The celebrated actor Alexander Moissi starred in one of his plays.

But Cracow also fell under the influence of the north. Stanisław Przybyszewski, the demon of modernism, friend of Strindberg and Munch, author of plays which enjoyed enormous success in Berlin and other German theatres, arrived in Cracow. Przybyszewski wrote with equal ease in Polish and German. He propagated the works of his famous Scandinavian friends and proclaimed a pessimistic outlook and total distrust in the world. The ideas he subscribed to were art for art's sake and complete decadence.

Under the direction of the noted authority of European literature Tadeusz Pawlikowski the Cracow theatre began to thrive again. In 1893 the theatre was moved into a new building worthy of Melpomene's glorious art, equipped with the latest stage machinery. All the latest European plays were produced here. The Cracow theatre presented Gorky's masterpiece *The Lower Depths* only a few months after its Moscow première. Plays by Ibsen and Chekhov were played here earlier and the plays of Strindberg, Hauptmann and Shaw made their appearance in the theatre's repertory.

Yet the importance of the Cracow theatre did not lie in these facts alone. More significant was the modernization that was taking place in the Polish theatre at the time. The developments occurring then were no more than the instruments, the arsenal of techniques, which would help the theatre attain its chief objectives: a national style for the Polish theatre, one that would be distinct and original and which would perhaps be more influential than the foreign avant-garde experiments in making a breakthrough. The man responsible for the developments and reforms in the theatre at the turn of the century was Stanisław Wyspiański.

He began to put the ideas of his programme into effect with the stage adaptation of *Forefathers' Eve* by Mickiewicz, the first production of the work anywhere. Wyspiański was guided in his experiments by Mickiewicz and his vision of the theatre. The premières of Wyspiański's original plays made a tremendous impact. *Wesele* (The Wedding) shook the entire Polish population to the core and *Wyzwolenie* (Liberation) remains to this day the most exciting discussion of the affairs of Poles. Although Wyspiański studied Shakespeare with great interest and though he wrote a profound and informed essay on Hamlet, yet he borrowed chiefly from the tradition of Polish folk art, from the puppet theatre, the nativity plays as well as from the works of the Polish Romantic poets. That is how the modern poetic epic drama developed and the theory of the theatre, which surprisingly foreshadowed Brecht's theories and practice many decades earlier, took form. Wyspiański either produced and directed his own plays or attended the rehearsals. He treated his plays as blueprints and designed the sets himself.

Wyspiański's preponderant influence on the Polish theatre is due to Leon Schiller, the greatest Polish stage director of the first half of the 20th century.

Schiller was born in Cracow in 1887. In his early youth he fell under the spell of Wyspiański and the Polish Romantic poets. At the same time, he was attracted by Polish folk art. During his travels across Europe, he met Gordon Craig and enthusiastically embraced his concepts of the theatre reform. He published a number of essays on the theatre in *The Mask*.

Schiller soon abandoned writing about the theatre for work in the theatre. In the beginning he was made literary director of the *Polski* Theatre of Warsaw, later he directed plays at Juliusz Osterwa's *Reduta* theatre. In 1924 he established the Bogusławski Theatre in Warsaw, together with Wilam Horzyca, writer and stage director, and two avant-garde artists, known as Formists (the Polish equivalent of Cubists), Andrzej and Zbigniew Pronaszko. A year later they were joined by the director and actor Aleksander Zelwerowicz.

The Bogusławski Theatre did not prosper long. The bourgeois government of interwar Poland looked with disfavour upon the activity of the avant-garde experiment and the decidedly left-wing repertory. Furthermore, the young arists could not cope with the mounting financial and administrative problems. Thus, it was no problem to push the theatre into bankruptcy. But the Bogusławski Theatre was the most important single manifestation of the militant poetic theatre of interwar Poland and Leon Schiller directed a few of the most important productions. They served to advance concepts of the theatre in the new social and political conditions which arose in Poland after it won its independence in 1918. Consequently, the theatre had through its. activity forged an important link between the theatre of Young Poland (Modernism) of the turn of the century and the theatre of People's Poland.

Leon Schiller's most important production at the Bogusławski Theatre was *Nie-Boska komedia* (The Undivine Comedy) by Zygmunt Krasiński. He brought out the revolutionary implications that lay hidden in the drama. Equally important was Stefan Żeromski's play on the 1905 revolution *Róża* (Rose) and Stanisław Wyspiański's *Achilleis* (Leon Schiller rarely directed Wyspiański's plays as if fearing he might succumb to the spellbinding power of that writer; on the other hand, he did not wish to be disloyal to his own principles) and finally Tadeusz Miciński's *Kniaź Potiomkin* (Prince Potemkin).

After the failure of the Bogusławski Theatre, Schiller repeated his experiment in Lvov where he headed a revolutionary poetic theatre in 1930—1931. He continued in the theatre as its principal stage director when his friend Wilam Horzyca took over the post of director. For a while Schiller worked with another leading Polish left-wing artist Stefan Jaracz, director of the *Ateneum* Theatre of Warsaw, which was housed in the Railwaymen's Trade Union building. There Schiller produced the widely known play *Roar, China* by the Soviet writer Serge Tretyakov. In the thirties Schiller evinced a lively interest in Erwin Piscator's political theatre and the theatre of fact. At this time too, Brecht's experiments struck a responsive chord. Schiller's production of *The Case of Sergeant Grischa* by Arnold Zweig, Wolf's *Cyanide* and Hašek's *The Good Soldier Schweik* reflect his new interests. A half year after the Berlin première, Schiller directed Brecht's *The Threepenny Opera* at the *Polski* Theatre in Warsaw. The types of plays directed by Schiller fall into three distinct categories: the song-plays based on old Polish songs — something on the order of first Polish musicals, contemporary plays with clear political implications and the great dramas of Polish Romantic and neo-romantic poets produced in the spirit of his vision of a monumental theatre. It is this last group of plays that made him famous and insured him a permanent position in the history of the Polish theatre.

After the last war, Schiller added to the golden series a fascinating production of Bogusławski's *The Cracovians and the Mountaineers* and Żeromski's *Sulkowski*. Although Schiller died in 1954, it might be said that he did his best work before the last war.

The period between the two wars witnessed a clash between two opposing tendencies in the theatre: psychological realism derived from the Moscow Art Theatre and poetic realism which remained under the influence of Polish Romantic and neo-romantic poets.

The latter trend was represented most fully by Leon Schiller. Psychological realism found its most brilliant expounder and advocate in the person of Juliusz Osterwa.

Juliusz Osterwa (1885—1947) was nearly the same age as Schiller. Like Schiller he grew up in Cracow under the influence of Wyspiański and the remarkable Cracow Theatre. He too made his first steps in the theatre in that city of poets, painters and scholars. But unlike Schiller, he won fame as an actor when still a very young man. When Schiller still served his apprenticeship to Craig, Osterwa was already the public idol of Cracow and Warsaw. Arnold Szyfman signed him up, together with a group of talented young actors of Cracow, when he established the *Polski* Theatre of Warsaw.

Szyfman, Osterwa, Jaracz, Węgrzyn and a few other leading actors of the *Polski* were Austrian citizens. When the war broke out in 1914, they were interned by the Russian authorities in Moscow where they remained safely throughout the war. The always energetic and enterprising Szyfman set up a Polish theatre in that city which gave the exiled actors not only a chance to earn a living but above all to develop their talents. Osterwa was therefore able to study the principles of Stanislavsky's theatre on the spot. Stanislavsky was on friendly terms with the Polish actors.

Upon his return to Poland, Osterwa decided to establish a theatre along the lines of the Moscow Art Theatre. We called it the *Reduta* (Redoubt). The ruling principles of the theatre were: the highest artistic standards and a complete renunciation of commercial goals. The creative ideas adopted by Osterwa were similar to Stanislavsky's. Thus, an in depth analysis of psychological motivations, emphasis on the work of the actor, less attention to the visual aspects of the production and more to the text which Osterwa considered the crucial component of a play.

Yet it was impossible not to see that Osterwa, together with his closest collaborator Mieczysław Limanowski, had put a distinctly Polish stamp on the Reduta. There was a peculiar duality in Osterwa. On the one hand, he was attracted by Stanislavsky's method and the technique of the Moscow Art Theatre and on the other he was fascinated most by Polish literature for the theatre. He loved Słowacki and gave a fabulous performance as Kordian and Fantazy, Słowacki's Romantic heroes. He was unrivaled in Zabłocki's comedy *The Dandy Goes A-courting* and was nuforgettable as the Prince in Calderon's drama as adapted by Słowacki. This sober realist, perceptive observer and remarkable organizer of the theatre was also a mystic. He was known to lie prostrate in church for hours. He must have been fascinated by the theatricality and ritual the church developed over the centuries.

There was something of the atmosphere of a monastic order about the *Reduta,* at any rate that was what Osterwa wanted it to be. As in Schiller's case, who while a Communist sympathizer and decidedly left wing in his political leanings in his creative work, paradoxically enough, stood close to the poetic mysteries, so we note a paradox in Osterwa. For while being a decided realist in his work in the theatre, he was at the same time a religious mystic and an enthusiast of Polish Romantic poetry. The line of development might be traced from Schiller to the work done by Kazimierz Dejmek and Adam Hanuszkiewicz and other representatives of the various versions of the Polish monumental theatre. The heirs of Osterwa and the *Reduta* are Jerzy Grotowski and his experimental Laboratory Theatre.

Schiller directed at the *Reduta* Theatre in the early days of its existence. But the two artists soon came to a parting of the ways. The actor Stefan Jaracz stayed longer with Osterwa but in the end he too went his way to establish the *Ateneum* Theatre where he remained faithful to psychological realism, though in his case it was more strongly tinged with left-wing political undertones. Jaracz was a civic minded artist. He believed that the theatre ought to play an active part in the affairs of the country.

The Polish theatre was not able to develop its potential in the years between the two world wars. It had to contend with financial difficulties and political problems. Theatre tickets were expensive and so the theatre could not count on mass attendance of the poorer classes. State support was meagre and paid out irregularly. It was necessary to pull strings and use influence. Theatres were leased out to managers or theatre companies who were granted subsidies (these not always honoured) and held responsible for the commercial success of the theatres. Consequently, the box office dictated the theatre repertory. The few plays of artistic repute were produced to preserve "the good name of the house."

Except for Schiller and Osterwa and a small group of gifted stage directors (Wierciński, Ziembiński, Węgierko, Radulski, Horzyca, Gall, Perzanowska), it was the actors, most of these first-rate artists, who were responsible for the reputation of the Polish theatre at this time. Next to the charismatic personality of Osterwa (who was more famous as an actor than a director), most noteworthy were Jaracz, withdrawn and forceful and endowed with a magnificent voice; Józef Węgrzyn, brilliant interpreter of Romantic roles; Aleksander Zelwerowicz, a great character actor most memorable perhaps as Porphyrus in *Crime and Punishment;* Kazimierz Junosza-Stępowski, technically perhaps the best Polish actor remarkable for his masterful delineation of character drawn with sharp precision and subtlety; Jerzy Leszczyński, noted for his natural and casual charm, invariably excellent in French comedies and superb in Fredro's plays, scion of a great family of actors; imperious and intimidating Stanisława Wysocka, the greatest tragedienne of the Polish stage. Other well known actors were the deeply touching Irena Solska and the legendary Ludwik Solski (who lived to a hundred after the Second World War, becoming one of the oldest actors in the world), Mieczysława Ćwiklińska and others.

Polish stage design of the interwar period was also of outstanding quality. Karol Frycz and Wincenty Drabik laid the foundations of Polish stage design at the *Polski* Theatre. The brothers Pronaszko contributed ideas derived from Cubism and Władysław Daszewski further enhanced it with his fresh pictorial vision and subtle colour composition producing a mood of contemplation tinged with irony.

Yet the theatre of the interwar period did not produce a uniform style. Nor did Polish drama flourish as it could have. The highly original plays of Stanisław Ignacy Witkiewicz passed almost unnoticed. One may speak only of individual productions, of remarkable directors, actors, stage designers and their work. One cannot say, however, that the Polish theatre was outstanding for its originality. It was overshadowed by the theatres founded by Stanislavsky and Meyerhold, Tairov and Vakhtangov, Piscator and Brecht, Artaud and Jouvet. The Polish muse of the theatre was finally able to speak in People's Poland.

CHAPTER III

THE THEATRE — YESTERDAY AND TODAY

The war years cruelly affected Poland and her culture. All the theatres were shut down, Leon Schiller, Stefan Jaracz and many prominent stage artists were imprisoned in the Nazi concentration camp at Auschwitz. Stage directors and actors died tragically, others lived in hiding, wasting the best years of their life, health and creative powers. The only Polish theatres operating at the time were in Lvov, Białystok and Vilna, cities then under Soviet administration. A number of Polish actors and stage directors found refuge here and were given a chance to work. But even these Polish theatres were disbanded when the war between the Third Reich and the Soviet Union broke out and the German troops invaded the territories of the Western Ukraine, Western Byelorussia and Lithuania. From then on the Polish theatres went underground, operating illegally in private homes. For more than five years Polish actors were deprived of the chance to get a formal education. Only a small conspiratorial school of the stage and a Secret Theatre Council were active in Poland during the war. The Council laid plans for the organization of theatres in postwar Poland.

Stefan Jaracz as Captain of Köpenick — caricature by Jerzy Zaruba

The Polish language was again heard from the stage in the summer of 1944, in Lublin and later in Rzeszów and Białystok, territories liberated in a massive Soviet offensive. The Polish Army Theatre arrived in Poland in the wake of the Soviet and Polish Armies. It had been organized in the USSR and was headed by stage director and actor Władysław Krasnowiecki who had escaped from Lvov before the invading German troops just in the nick of time. The theatre played Fredro's *Śluby panieńskie* (Maidens' Vows) in Lublin to an enthusiastic audience starved for the Polish language and theatre. Next, Krasnowiecki presented Wyspiański's *The Wedding* in liberated Cracow. Finally, however, he as Leon Schiller, settled in Łódź. Schiller came to Łódź soon as he was set free from the German concentration camp and soon headed the Polish Army Theatre. It is to him that the theatre owes its postwar development. Juliusz Osterwa also found himself in Łódź after the war and shortly after the liberation of the city put on Słowacki's *Fantazy*. The finest artists of the Polish stage congregated in Łódź in those years. Apart from Schiller and Osterwa there was also Aleksander Zelwerowicz and Józef Węgrzyn. Edmund Wierciński directed *Electra* by Giraudoux in which Zelwerowicz turned in a marvellous performance. Schiller directed such memorable productions as Bogusławski's *The Cracovians and the Mountaineers*, Shakespeare's *The Tempest*, *Celestina* by Rojas, Drda's *Playing with the Devil* and Gorky's *The Lower Depths*. He surrounded himself with his former associates and a group of new pupils. The theatre suffered a grave loss when Stefan Jaracz died of tuberculosis in 1945. He left the Polish actors a fine legacy of the ideological function of the theatre. Absent as well was Aleksander Węgierko, murdered by the

Nazi occupation authorities and Mieczysław Węgrzyn who died in Auschwitz. Still around and active in the theatre were Karol Adwentowicz, Władysław Daszewski, Jacek Woszczerowicz and many other leading artists who had won recognition before the war. A theatre school opened in Łódź and everything seemed to indicate that the period of reconstruction had got off to a good start.

Cracow rose to second rank as a theatre centre. Many of the leading stage artists fled to Cracow after the Warsaw Uprising. Juliusz Osterwa left Łódź to become director of the Cracow theatre. When premature death cut short his activity in 1947, Bronisław Dąbrowski, *pro tem.* director of the Katowice theatre, took over the management of the Cracow theatre. He brought with him a group of talented artists, notable among whom were Władysław Krzemiński, Tadeusz Kondrat, Tadeusz Surowa and others. Andrzej Pronaszko, with whom Dąbrowski worked in Katowice, was appointed stage designer of the Cracow theatre. The theatre company was further strengthened when Jan Kurnakowicz joined the theatre. Local talent, young and old, began to make its mark. There was a flurry of promising debuts. Kazimierz Opaliński came into his own as Menge in Lope de Vega's *Sheep well,* consolidating his position with an equally fine portrayal of Chebutikin in *The Three Sisters* by Chekhov. Zofia Rysiówna made a striking appearance as Balladyna and then as Diana in *Fantazy,* sharing honours with Juliusz Osterwa. Aleksandra Śląska and Halina Mikołajska, Tadeusz Łomnicki, Gustaw Holoubek and many other artists who were to play such an important part in the life of the Polish theatre made their debuts here.

The period of twenty-five years of People's Poland

may be divided into the following four periods: 1944—1949 — the reconstruction of the Polish theatre after the devastations of war; 1949—1954 — offensive of a new theme; 1955—1962 — repairing of mistakes and opening the door to the world; 1963—1970 — creative work in the great national classics, development of a Polish style of drama and theatre.

Most pressing in the first period was resumption of work in the theatre in the entire country. It was necessary to open again the theatres that had existed before the war and to set up new ones where there had been none before. To illustrate the point, we might take Cracow as an example. Before the war Cracow had a single theatre which did not draw a very high attendance. Premières were held every week or at best every two weeks. After the Second World War, it was necessary to establish five theatres in Cracow. Many of the plays were performed as many as a hundred times (to capacity audiences). Today Cracow has nine resident theatre companies.

The new postwar theatre was created by a cadre of artists painfully decimated by the war. Though the obstacles were enormous yet they were surmounted in the end. By 1945 nearly all the major cultural and administrative centres of the country had their theatres. Not only Warsaw, Łódź, Cracow, Poznań, Lublin, Rzeszów, Białystok and Katowice but also Olsztyn and Gdańsk, Wrocław and Jelenia Góra, Opole and Szczecin. Such small towns as Chorzów and Świdnica also got a theatre.

In Warsaw, Arnold Szyfman took charge of clearing up the debris and of supervising the reconstruction of the *Polski* Theatre building. He set to work with his usual energy. Fortunately, the building was not seriously damaged and so in January 1946, on the first anniversary of the liberation of Warsaw, the most popular theatre of the capital opened its doors to the public. The theatre inaugurated its activities in the new Poland with Słowacki's *Lilla Weneda,* starring the young Elżbieta Barszczewska in the title role.

What was seen in the Polish theatres at the time? First of all, Polish and other classics. It was necessary to introduce the thousands of new theatregoers, who got their first taste of the theatre after the war, to the masterpieces of Polish and world literature. The audiences were composed not only of young people who had been unable to attend the theatre in the years of war but also of older persons to whom the doors of the theatre had been shut before the revolution and the emergence of social changes after the war. The classics offered excellent stage training to young actors who had just come to the theatre — and there were many of them. As they had no formal training in acting, they had to learn by practice. Although the theatres played Słowacki and Wyspiański, Lope de Vega's *Sheep well* and Molière's *L'Ecole des Femmes,* yet most frequently produced were the comedies of the most popular Polish author Aleksander Fredro, the commedies of manner of Gabriela Zapolska and the plays of Shakespeare.

The first major test of the reborn Polish theatre in the early postwar years, the first proving ground of its talents and quality, was the 1947 Shakespearean Festival. Theatres from all parts of the country (and not only from the major cultural centres) took part in the festival. The jury was composed of prominent authorities on the theatre from Poland and other countries, notable among whom was Tyrone Guthrie. The thirteen theatres that took part in the festival presented nine plays of

Shakespeare. The first group prize went to the *Wybrzeże* Theatre for *As You Like It* directed by Iwo Gall who also received one of the major individual prizes for direction. The first prize in that department went to Leon Schiller for his direction of *The Tempest* with stage design by Władysław Daszewski (who also won a prize) and with Karol Adwentowicz appearing as Prospero. Other prizes went to Wilam Horzyca for *Romeo and Juliet*, directing the Toruń theatre company, Andrzej Pronaszko for stage design to *A Midsummer Night's Dream*, directed by Bronisław Dąbrowski in Cracow; Karol Frycz for the sets to *Hamlet* produced by *Polski* Theatre of Warsaw; Wojciech Brydziński for his performance as the Old Actor in the same play and to Feliks Krassowski for his sets to *The Taming of the Shrew*. A total of nineteen prizes and thirteen other awards were distributed. Some of the most noteworthy performances seen during the festival were given by Jan Kurnakowicz as Bottom in *A Midsummer Night's Dream*, Elżbieta Barszczewska as Ophelia in *Hamlet* and Marian Wyrzykowski in the title role in the same play.

Shakespeare's plays were produced outside the festival as well. Most memorable were *Twelfth Night* directed by Bronisław Dąbrowski with sets by Andrzej Stopka and starring Maria Kościałkowska as Puck, Tadeusz Łomnicki as the Jester and Stanisław Jaworski as Malvolio.

It would be wrong to claim that there were no contemporary plays in the repertory of the Polish theatre at the time. On the contrary, every theatre held premières of new works by contemporary Polish authors as well as first Polish productions of interesting plays from other countries. Most significant from the perspective of time seems Jerzy Szaniawski's *Dwa Teatry* (Two Theatres) which opened on February 24th, 1946 at the *Powszechny* Theatre in Cracow. The play was directed by Irena Grywińska, with Karol Adwentowicz in the principal role. Soon afterwards the play was put on by the Katowice theatre, remarkably directed by Edmund Wierciński and with sets by Andrzej Pronaszko. The play broached for the first time a problem that is fundamental to the development of the Polish theatre; it gave a confrontation between the ideas of a naturalistic and a poetic theatre skillfully packed into a single performance. Szaniawski called the first the "Little Looking Glass" theatre and the second "the Theatre of Dreams." He pitted poetic reverie against what came to be known as "the little realism." There was no doubt where the author's sentiments lay. With his usual subtle irony he ridiculed the warped attitude of the theatre, he called the "Little Looking Glass," arguing that following the atrocities of the last war, the theatre must devote itself to daydreams and reverie. By seeking to break the narrow confines of the naturalistic theatre restricted to domestic drama, Szaniawski remained faithful to Wyspiański's teachings. The years that followed were not all smooth sailing for the *Two Theatres* and its author. In the end, however, time proved him right. The poetic theatre triumphed in Poland and the *Two Theatres* is played with success on the Polish stage to this day. Erwin Axer revived the play in 1969 at the *Współczesny* Theatre of Warsaw and directed it at the Gorky Theatre of Leningrad. The play and the productions aroused public interest in Poland and the Soviet Union.

But *Two Theatres* was not the only play to enjoy success at the time. The *Stary* (Old) Theatre of Cracow inaugurated its postwar activity on March 31st, 1945 with the first performance of Jerzy Zawieyski's new metaphorical play on Job called *Mąż doskonały* (The Ideal Husband), directed by Jerzy Ronard-Bujański, with sets by Andrzej Pronaszko and starring Edmund Wierciński and Zofia Małynicz. The *Stary* of Cracow next produced two other plays by Zawieyski: *Masław* and *Rozdroże miłości* (The Crossroads of Love), a play concerned with the moral problems that arise when a priest falls in love. The play owed its tremendous success principally to the performance of Zofia Rysiówna and Władysław Hańcza. Cracow was a veritable seedbed of contemporary Polish drama. Among the plays which received their first performances here were: *Dom pod Oświęcimiem* (A House Near Auschwitz), a new play by Tadeusz Hołuj (the play was also produced by the *Polski* Theatre of Warsaw); Świrszczyńska's *Orpheus* which, though it opened earlier at Toruń, is remarkable for the fact that it marked the success of Halina Mikołajska in the Cracow production; *Noe i jego menażeria* (Noah and His Menagerie), a first play by Tadeusz Łomnicki; *Wielkanoc* (Easter) by Stefan Otwinowski, *Zamach* (The Assassination) by Tadeusz Breza and Stanisław Dygat, *Powrót syna marnotrawnego* (Return of the Prodigal Son), a play about Rembrandt, the best of Roman Brandstaetter's plays directed by Janusz Warnecki who also played the leading role and with striking sets by Karol Frycz. The Cracow theatre also produced Leon Kruczkowski's first postwar play *Odwety* (Retaliations), which received its first performance by the *Polski* Theatre of Warsaw, and Juliusz Wirski's *Cement*, a play with clear political implications.

In Łódź, the theatres played *Papuga* (The Parrot) and

Bankiet (The Banquet) by Kazimierz Korcelli, the Katowice theatre produced Ludwik Hieronim Morstin's *Taniec księżniczki* (The Dance of the Princess) and the *Wybrzeże* Theatre produced Gajcy's *Homer and Orchid*. Also produced at this time were the new plays of Stefan Flukowski and Adam Grzymała-Siedlecki, while in Warsaw Wacław Kubacki's *Krzyk jarzębiny* (The Cry of the Rowan Tree), a play about Słowacki's friend Spitznagel, and Michał Rusinek's *Kobieta we mgle* (Woman in the Mist), with a memorable performance by Maria Gorczyńska, enjoyed a deserved triumph.

The Polish theatres did not turn their backs on the new foreign plays. Erwin Axer produced at the *Kameralny* Theatre of Łódź: Tennessee Williams' *The Glass Menagerie* with Zofia Mrozowska turning in a memorable performance; *La P... respectueuse* by Sartre, starring Ewa Bonacka, *The Winslow Boy* by Terence Rattigan and Maxwell Anderson's *Joan of Lorraine,* starring Irena Eichler. Axer thus presented completely unknown authors to the Polish audiences. In Cracow Janusz Warnecki produced Jean Anouilh's *Passenger Without Luggage* in which he gave a fine performance as the leading character. Priestley's mystery *An Inspector Calls* was produced by a few theatres. Maria Dulęba was a sensation in Peyrest-Chappuis *The Late Monsieur Pik*. The plays of Giraudoux were the rage. Maria Dulęba gave an excellent performance in *The Madwomen of Chaillot* in Cracow, Łódź flocked to see *Electra* and *Amphitryon 38* played with equal success in other cities. Polish audiences were able to see Armand Salacrou's *Nights of Anger* and the *Lenoir Archipelago* as well as Arthur Miller's first play *All My Sons.*

Soviet drama was represented principally by the plays of Constantine Simonov. *The Russians* was performed by a remarkable cast that included Solski, Leszczyński and Siemaszkowa and *The Russian Question* (produced under the more striking title *Harry Smith Discovers America*) was directed by Władysław Krzemiński, starring Jan Kurnakowicz, Tadeusz Białoszczyński and Tadeusz Kondrat. Seen at the time was the witty comedy by Petrov called *Island of Peace*. In Toruń Wilam Horzyca produced Yesenin's *Pugachov* while in Katowice Władysław Krasnowiecki directed and played the title role of Gorky's *Yegor Buliczev and the Others* and Mayakovsky's *Good*. Czech plays were received with enthusiasm thanks to Leon Schiller's inspired production of Drda's *Playing with the Devil* at the Łódź Theatre, with imaginative sets by Otto Axer and starring Stanisław Łapiński and Feliks Żukowski, both displaying great comic talent — the first as the brigand Sarka Farka and the second as the brave soldier Marcin Kabat.

This fine beginning was slowed down by the sudden changes in cultural policies. The programme of socialist realism was proclaimed in January 1949 as the reigning style in all fields of art, hence also in the theatre, at the Congress of the Polish Writers' Union held in Szczecin. Pressure was applied for changes in the repertory and an all out war was declared on what was called formalism, though no one was quite certain what it meant or how it should be defined. The intentions that guided the architects of the new cultural policies were undoubtedly justified while the principles formulated could in given circumstances be of benefit to the Polish theatre by enlivening and galvanizing it. For the idea was to stimulate the theatre to present plays on contemporary topics and to cause it to establish closer contact with the life of People's Poland and its problems as well as with the new public. Unfortunately, the methods used to put these policies into effect were fumbling and inept, consequently the objective was not attained.

The beginning of the new period did not foreshadow failure. Bohdan Korzeniowski directed a striking production of Fredro's *Mąż i żona* (Man and Wife) at the *Kameralny* Theatre of Warsaw with an all star cast including Janina Romanówna, Justyna Kreczmar, Jan Kreczmar and Czesław Wołłejko. In Poznań, Irena Eichlerówna appeared in Racine's *Phèdre* directed by Wilam Horzyca and with sets by Jan Kosiński. The première of Leon Kruczkowski's *Niemcy* (The Germans) was held at the *Stary* Theatre of Cracow on October 22nd, 1949, directed by Bronisław Dąbrowski. The play was received with enthusiasm and was acclaimed an important work of contemporary Polish drama. Soon afterwards, the play was directed by Erwin Axer at the *Współczesny* Theatre of Warsaw and a few weeks later it opened at the Deutsches Theatre of Berlin, featuring the talented actor Paul Bildt in the leading role. The play was produced by Polish, German and Czech theatres. The *Nowy* Theatre, later known as the Dejmek Theatre, inaugurated its activities on November 12th, 1949 with a play by the Czech writer Vasek Kana *Brigade of the Grinder Karhan*. Set in a factory among workers, the play dealt with social conflict that was both crucial to the times and sharply drawn. The young cast, headed by Kazimierz Dejmek, played with moving earnestness. They were ably abetted by such experienced actors of the older generation as Stanisław Łapiński and Józef Pilarski. The opening was a momentous evening marking the young company's revolt against the absence of ideals in the theatre and its desire to put into effect a militant programme of art, of a socialist art.

The Festival of Russian and Soviet Plays injected new vigour into the life of the Polish theatre. The idea of the festival was put forward at the Congress of the Polish-Soviet Friendship Society. It was the biggest theatre festival ever organized in Poland and was to play a crucial role in the life of the Polish theatre. All the theatres and nearly all the leading artists of the theatre took part in it. Thus, 47 theatres presented a total of 60 plays. Twenty-seven of the theatres and 30 plays were qualified for the finals, offering a wide and diversified review of Russian and Soviet plays in productions of the highest quality. The dramatist Leon Kruczkowski chaired the jury which awarded the group prizes. Recipients of the prizes were: the dramatic theatres of Cracow for their productions of Chekhov's *Three Sisters* and Trenev's *Lubov Yerovaya* directed by Bronisław Dąbrowski and with stage sets by Andrzej Stopka and the *Narodowy* Theatre of Warsaw for Gorky's *Yegor Bulichev and the Others* directed by Władysław Krasnowiecki and stage designs by Władysław Daszewski. In the department of stage direction prizes went to: Bronisław Dąbrowski for *Three Sisters*, Władysław Krasnowiecki for *Yegor Buliczev* and Leon Schiller for *The Lower Depths*. Prizes were awarded to the following stage designers: Władysław Daszewski, Otto Axer and Andrzej Stopka. The first prizes for performance were voted for Jan Kurnakowicz, Jacek Woszczerowicz, Aleksander Zelwerowicz, Kazimierz Opaliński and Zdzisław Karczewski. The leading stage artists came off best in all areas. Among the best portrayals we might recall Władysław Krasnowiecki as Yegor Bulichev, Jan Kurnakowicz as Shvandia and Pokolesin, Kazimierz Opaliński as Chebutikin, Mieczysława Ćwiklińska as Fiolka in Gogol's *Marriage*, Jacek

Woszczerowicz as Tarelkin and Jan Świderski's great performance as the Baron in *The Lower Depths*. *Three Sisters* featured the young artists Zofia Rysiówna — an unforgettable Masha, Halina Mikołajska — a deeply moving Irina, Tadeusz Łomnicki and others. Gustaw Holoubek won acclaim as Pershykhin in the Katowice production of *The Townsfolk*. All in all, it was a successful festival.

Polish theatres gave a number of excellent productions of other Russian and Soviet plays. Notable among these was Ostrovsky's *Wolves and Sheep* and Gorky's *The Enemies* at the *Polski* Theatre of Warsaw, *The Cocks Crow* by Lithuanian writer Baltushis directed by Bohdan Korzeniewski and stage design by Andrzej Pronaszko, featuring Seweryna Broniszówna, Jan Świderski, Hanna Skarżanka, Jacek Woszczerowicz and Ryszarda Hanin was given at the *Kameralny* Theatre and finally the Polish première of Griboedov's *Wit Works Woe* was directed by Bronisław Dąbrowski at the *Polski* Theatre with a cast which included Jan Kurnakowicz, Jan Kreczmar, Elżbieta Barszczewska and Justyna Kreczmar.

Polish and world classics were not neglected either. There was the truly impressive production of Fredro's *Zemsta* (The Revenge) at the *Narodowy* Theatre, directed by Bohdan Korzeniewski, with Jan Kurnakowicz as Cup-bearer and Jacek Woszczerowicz as Papkin. The *Narodowy* Theatre presented an expert production of *The Dandy Goes A-courting* with Czesław Wołłejko, Hanna Skarżanka and Andrzej Szczepkowski. In Wrocław, Edmund Wierciński directed Shakespeare's *As You Like It* with Ewa Krasnodębska as Rosalind. Maria Wiercińska adapted the nearly forgotten *Comedy* by Apollo Korzeniowski, father of Joseph Conrad, and Fredro's

Maidens' Vows. The Wrocław production of Bogusław-
ski's *Henry IV at the Chase* won high critical acclaim.
In Warsaw, Bohdan Korzeniewski directed Molière's
Don Juan, with Jan Kreczmar in the title role and Jacek
Woszczerowicz as Sganarel.

Russian dramas were represented by an excellent
production of Gogol's *Revizor* at the *Narodowy* Theatre,
with Jan Kurnakowicz as the perfect embodiment of
the Khorodnichy (Town Bailiff) and Tolstoy's *Fruit of
Education* at the Słowacki Theatre of Cracow directed
by Władysław Krzemiński. Jakub Rotbaum directed
Pogodin's *Man with a Gun*. This was the first time Lenin was impersonated on the Polish stage. Leon Schiller
directed what was to be his last play at the *Polski* Theatre. It was *The Armoured Train* by Vsevolod Ivanov,
with stage design by Andrzej Pronaszko. *Uncle Vanya*
at the Kameralny Theatre was also well done, with fine
portrayals by Witold Różycki as Serebryakov, Elżbieta
Barszczewska as Helen and Ryszarda Hanin as Sonya.

Yet this period ended in failure. There were several
reasons for this. The Festival of Contemporary Polish
Plays, organized in 1951, put a damper on the development of the Polish Theatre. With the relaxed standards,
bad and very bad plays were admitted so long as they
dealt with problems and followed the stereotypes of
plot acceptable to the organizers. A total of thirty plays
was accepted, some of these testifying to outright inep-
titude. Pressure was applied on the theatres to produce
these plays thus putting the festival and contemporary
Polish drama in bad odour and compromising the reputation of the Polish theatre itself. The weakness of the
plays and of the theatre compounded the evil. The more
strongly established theatres either chose the best plays
of the lot or did not take part in the festival if they did

not find a play that met their requirement. The weaker theatres simply had to take the plays forced on them by the Ministry of Culture and Art. The resulting productions, by virtue of the indifferent staging and acting, emphasized the weak points of the texts.

Another reason for the decline of the Polish theatre at the time was the centralized administration under which the theatres were put. Art directors of the individual theatres were thus deprived of the last vestige of independence and the right to follow their individual bent or to conduct creative explorations. The more rigid and dogmatic the interpretation of the standard rules and injunctions of socialist realism, the more painful the burden imposed on the theatres. Things came to such a pass at length that it was impossible to produce even the plays of Leon Kruczkowski, leading author of People's Poland and chairman of the Writers' Union. He came out with a sharp criticism of the outcome of the Festival of Contemporary Polish Plays. But precisely when restrictions on dramatic literature were the most onerous, new (and encouraging) symptoms began to appear.

An important influence was exercised by the guest appearances of foreign theatres in Poland. The Okhlopkov Theatre arrived in Warsaw in 1949 with Fadeyev's *The Young Guard* proving that there was greater freedom in the Soviet Union as regards the artistic form of stage productions than the home-grown interpreters and defenders of socialist realism imagined. In 1951, the Pushkin Theatre of Leningrad brought its admirable production of Tolstoy's *The Living Corpse* with Simonov giving a brilliant portrayal of the leading character. This production, too, did not hold to the canons of socialist realism. In the final months of 1952, the Berliner

Ensemble of Brecht came to Warsaw with its world famous production of *Mother Courage and Her Children* knocking down the whole rigid structure of ideas on the theatre. The majority of critics viewed Brecht's theatre with enormous interest and acclaim, and despite the official opinion of some of the powers that be, placed high value on the originality and excellence of his plays. Opinion was further consolidated on a different interpretation of socialist realism following the guest appearance of the Mossoviet Theatre and the imaginative staging of Lermontov's *Masquarade* and primarily after the appearance of the Vakhtangov Theatre in an exciting production of Gorky's *Yegor Bulichev and Others.* When the Théàtre National Populaire arrived in Warsaw in 1954 with its poetic interpretations of *Le Cid, Ruy Blas* and *Don Juan* the ground had been prepared for its reception. The Polish public sensed that this poetic realism reflected what they felt and so warmly applauded Gerard Philipe, Jean Vilar and Daniel Sorano. These facts could not fail to have their effect on the further development of the Polish theatre.

Meanwhile, in Moscow, Mayakowsky's *The Bath* returned to the stage to once again lash out at bureaucracy with the sharp edge of satire. In Poland, Kazimierz Dejmek cherished the idea of producing the play at the *Nowy* Theatre of Łódź for a number of years. And so Mayakovsky's comedy opened on December 11th, 1954 and scored an immediate success. The theatre was then invited to Warsaw where the production aroused general public enthusiasm.

The period of the renewal of the Polish theatre, the third period in the history of the postwar theatre, concentrated on righting the errors and on making up for lost time. For a number of years the Polish theatre had been completely cut off from other countries and information of what was going on there. Now the door to the world stood open again. New plays, the good and the bad, of western writers found their way to Poland. It was difficult to make a wise selection, great caution had to be practiced. What should have been a source of strength became for a time the cause of chaos and weakness. Kazimierz Dejmek, more than any other director, pursued his own programme without looking to changing trends and fads. After *The Bath,* he directed *Święto Winkelrieda* (Feast of Winkelried) by Andrzejewski and Zagórski, a play which though written during the war lost none of its immediacy even now. The third play in the series was the stage adaptation of Andrzejewski's novel *Ciemności kryją ziemię* (The Inquisitors). The Holy Inquisition was made the symbol of matters far closer to home and pertaining to the personality cult.

One of the most painful and most harmful restrictions of the preceding period was the injunction against the production of the masterpieces of Polish national literature, of the great works of Romantic and neo-romantic poets which constituted everything that was valuable and treasured in Polish drama. These injunctions were now revoked. To mark the centenary of the death of Adam Mickiewicz, the *Polski* Theatre of Warsaw gave the first post war production of *Forefathers' Eve* directed by Aleksander Bardini. Soon afterwards Erwin Axer directed *Kordian* at the *Narodowy* (National) Theatre with lovely sets designed by Władysław Daszewski and with Tadeusz Łomnicki in the title role. After an absence of seven years, Wyspiański's *The Wedding* returned to the Polish stage. In 1955, the new theatre in the Palace of Culture and Sciences in Warsaw, inaugurated its activities with a production of the play. The theatre was later named the *Dramatyczny* (Dramatic) Theatre of the Capital City of Warsaw. Krasiński's *Nie-Boska komedia* (Undivine Comedy) opened at the *Nowy* Theatre of Łódź on June 19th, 1959. The play was directed by Bohdan Korzeniewski with stage designs by Józef Szajna. The broader knowledge of Polish dramas gained at this time was due not only to the repeal of the injunctions in force, but also thanks to the new and creative readings given by Polish directors which uncovered new ground. The leader in this area was Kazimierz Dejmek, with his splendid staging of the ancient Polish dramas at the *Nowy* Theatre of Łódź: namely *Life of Joseph* and *the History of the Lord's Glorious Resurrection.*

Another encouraging development in this new period was the progressing decentralization of life in the theatre. The central administration released a number of agencies connected with theatres to the local national councils. The directors of theatres gained greater independence and, what goes with it, initiative and a sense of responsibility. The atmosphere was favourable to the formation of companies with a clearly defined ideological and artistic image and the individualization of theatres. The most ambitious of these pursued their own concepts. Not all the theatres were able to give up the eclectic repertory and not all were capable of developing an individual style. In cities with one theatre, the one stage was expected to fulfil many roles and could not confine its activities to a single area of interest. In larger cultural centres and in cases where an outstanding artistic personality attracted people who subscribed to the same ideas and programme, the crystallization of distinct ideological and artistic attitudes could be observed.

This was true of the *Nowy* Theatre of Łódź. From the beginning of its existence the theatre developed a distinct style. The same was true of the *Ludowy* Theatre at Nowy Huta, headed by Krystyna Skuszanka and Jerzy Krasowski working together with the gifted stage designer Józef Szajna. The *Dramatyczny* Theatre of the capital city of Warsaw belonged to the same category. Here, Marian Miller as administrative director managed to attract a group of talented artists who formulated the ideological and artistic programme of that theatre. Other theatres began to develop individual styles as well. First among these was the *Współczesny* Theatre of Warsaw, headed by Erwin Axer. Under his guidance it became preeminent in the field of contemporary plays, with an excellent company of actors and an imaginative leadership. Among these, next to Axer, was the noted authority of contemporary literature and perceptive stage director Jerzy Kreczmar, the dramatist and editor-in-chief of the theatre monthly *Dialog* Adam Tarn (who was literary director of the *Współczesny* Theatre at the time) and editor-in-chief of the biweekly *Teatr* Edward Csató who, though he was not on the staff of the *Współczesny,* willingly offered advice.

Decentralization became a stimulating factor in theatre life in smaller centres as well. The theatres of Cracow and Łódź occupied only a slightly inferior position to the Warsaw theatres although there were times when the Cracow and Łódź theatres successfully challenged the theatres of the capital for priority. The exodus of many provincial actors to Warsaw in 1949—1955, weakened the Cracow theatres more gravely than others. Now we observe a clear strengthening of the position of the Cracow theatres. Bronisław Dąbrowski, who in the preceding period performed the difficult and demanding functions of the director of the *Polski* Theatre of Warsaw, now returned to his post as director of the Słowacki Theatre in Cracow. Władysław Krzemiński assumed the post of director of the *Stary* Theatre and raised it to a high artistic level. Life quickened in the theatres of Wrocław and the Coast. Zygmunt Hübner emerged on the coast in the late fifties as a forceful personality, developing into one of the best art directors in Poland. Marek Okopiński organized an interesting theatre at Zielona Góra which was soon to become famous in all of Poland. The Wyspiański Theatre of Katowice flourished under the directorship of Jerzy Kaliszewski. It was here that Jerzy Jarocki won his first success as stage designer. Decentralization continued in depth.

The Polish theatres could not be satisfied with classics alone at a time when the political and social life of the country was so lively and dynamic. In the second half of the fifties, People's Poland was emerging in a new form to replace the model of the years of "the personality cult." Contemporary Polish drama and the Polish theatre wished to participate in the general national debate. The writers and the theatres realized that this is the kind of plays and productions the people wanted to see. The critics were also aware of this when they rose to defend Jerzy Lutowski's *Ostry dyżur* (Night Duty), produced at the *Narodowy* Theatre of Warsaw in 1955. The theatres once again turned to plays by authors from socialist countries, with great interest

---

Jacek Woszczerowicz as Richard III — caricature by Adam Perzyk

shown in the works of Mayakovsky. This interest proved of benefit to ideology and art. Among the best productions seen at this time were: *The Caucasian Chalk Circle* directed by Irena Babel at the Słowacki Theatre of Cracow with stage sets done in the Polish highland folk art style by Andrzej Stopka; there was the noteworthy production of *The Good Woman of Setzuan* at the *Dramatyczny* of Warsaw, directed by Ludwik René with stage designs by Jan Kosiński and with Halina Mikołajska in the title role. In Łódź, Tadeusz Minc directed *Galileo*, finally *The Resistible Rise of Arturo Ui*, directed by Erwin Axer, with Tadeusz Łomnicki in the title role, was a signal success.

The picture would not be complete if we failed to mention the Western plays (some of them existentialist) which arrived in Poland after 1955. After years of nearly total isolation, it was understandable that the audiences as well as the theatre artists were curious about that literature. After so many years there was much to choose from. There are no more than a few, and at time only one or two, really good plays produced in the world each year. In 1955 and over the next few years, the Polish theatre had over a dozen remarkable plays and over a score of very good plays to choose from. The immediate results were good because the theatres could improve the quality of their repertory and attract wide interest in the theatre. At the same time, more was demanded of the theatres.

Beckett's *Waiting for Godot*, the most celebrated play of the theatre of the absurd, received a fine production at the *Współczesny* Theatre. Jerzy Kreczmar, the director of the play, sought to find and bring out points where Beckett's play coincided with Polish issues, an undertaking in which he was successful in some

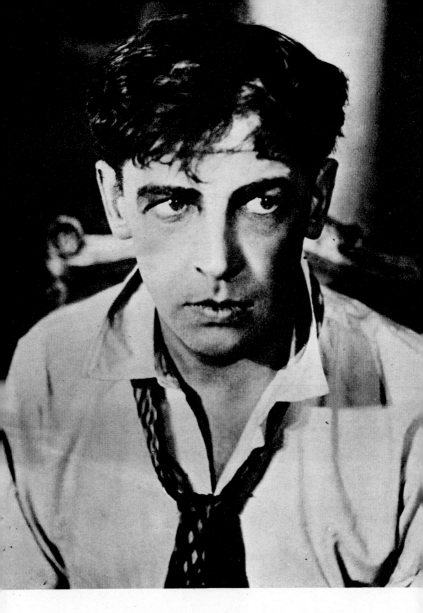

Juliusz Osterwa (1885—1947), one of the greatest Polish actors, director of *Reduta*, hero of the Polish Romantic and Neo-Romantic drama

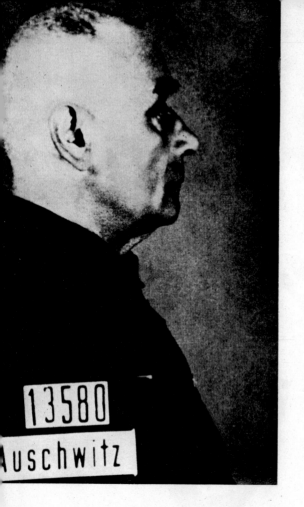

13580
Auschwitz

Stefan Jaracz (1883—1945), remarkable actor, founder of the *Ateneum* Theatre, prisoner of Auschwitz

Barbara Krafftówna and Wojciech Siemion in a scene from Mikołaj Rej's *The Life of Joseph*, staged and directed by Kazimierz Dejmek

Leon Schiller (1887—1953), the most eminent Polish stage director of the first half of the 20th century, proponent of the concept of the poetic monumental theatre, founder and for many years dean of the Department of Stage Direction at the State Theatre School

Jacek Woszczerowicz as Richard III

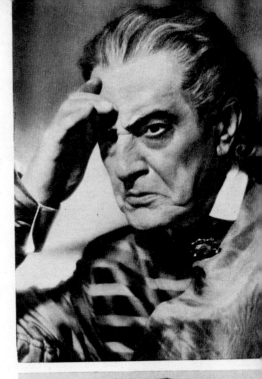

Jerzy Leszczyński (1884—1959) as Hetman Kossakowski in *Horsztyński* by Juliusz Słowacki

Kazimierz Dejmek, author of the famous productions of Polish plays, for many years director of the *Narodowy* Theatre in Warsaw

Antoni Różycki and Zbigniew Sawan in a scene from Fredro's
Man and Wife

Halina Mikołajska as Irina, Celina Niedźwiecka as Olga and
Zofia Rysiówna as Masha in Chekhov's *Three Sisters* at the
Słowacki Theatre of Cracow, with Bronisław Dąbrowski as stage
director and Andrzej Stopka as stage designer

Hamlet at the Horzyca Theatre of Toruń directed by Jan Maciejowski, stage sets by Zofia Wierchowicz and with Marek Bargiełowski in the title role

Erwin Axer, leading Polish stage director, heads the *Współczesny* Theatre of Warsaw

degree. An adaptation of Kafka's *The Trial* was presented at the Ateneum Theatre with an admirable portrayal given by Jacek Woszczerowicz. The *Dramatyczny* Theatre of Warsaw presented Ionesco's *Les Chaises* (The Chairs), with Halina Mikołajska and Jan Świderski, directed by Ludwik René, turning this farce into a tragedy of existence, an interpretation that imbued it with a semblance of timeliness. The same theatre gave a première of Sartre's *Le Diable et le Bon Dieu,* in which Gustaw Holoubek, one of the most eminent of Polish actors, scored a signal success as Goetz. The *Dramatyczny* Theatre achieved its greatest triumph by discovering the plays of Dürrenmatt. The success of Dürrenmatt's *The Visit* directed by Ludwik René and with sets by Jan Kosiński, opened the door of all the Polish theatres to the plays of the Swiss dramatist for many years to come.

I do not know whether Dürrenmatt's plays are as popular in any other European country as they are in Poland. The *Dramatyczny* Theatre produced one of his plays every year. The Warsaw productions were usually followed by others in the country. The following plays were produced: *Romulus the Great, The Angel Descended to Babylon, Frank V, The Physicists, The Anabaptists, Meteor* and *King John.* The *Współczesny* Theatre added to the series a very good production of *Play Strindberg,* directed by Andrzej Wajda. At the *Współczesny* Theatre, Erwin Axer directed *The Firebugs* by Frisch, while the *Ateneum* presented his *Andorra* and *Biography.* Yet surprisingly enough the plays of the author of *Gantenbein* never won the recognition accorded to the works of Dürrenmatt. It is undoubtedly the *Dramatyczny* Theatre, called sometimes the Dürrenmatt Theatre, which made that author's reputation in the country.

It is not possible to list all the plays of Western authors seen on the Polish stage from the latter part of the fifties, through the sixties and the early seventies. Notable among these were: Beckett's *Happy Days* and *Endgame;* Ionesco's *Le Rhinocéros* and *Exit the King;* Pinter's *The Caretaker, The Birthday Party* and *The Dumb Waiter;* Osborne's *Look Back in Anger, The Entertainer* and *Inadmissible Evidence; Tennessee* Williams' *A Streetcar Named Desire, Orpheus Descending* and *The Night of the Iguana;* Arthur Miller's *Death of a Salesman, The Crucible, After the Fall* and *Incident at Vichy;* Edward Albee's *Who's Afraid of Virginia Woolf?, Tiny Alice* and *Everything in the Garden.* There were also productions of plays by Sean O'Casey, John Arden, Shelagh Delaney and of many plays of Anouilh. The claim may be made that there was not a single outstanding play that was not produced by a Polish theatre.

There were certain advantages to this development. Polish artists (directors, actors and set designers) were able to learn of the new trends and means of expression that prevailed in contemporary drama and the contemporary theatre. At the same time, they were able to compare their own experiences, knowledge about the theatre and practice with the new developments in the theatre. The technique and the arsenal of means of expression was greatly enriched in these years. But there was another side to the issue. The influx of such a great number of good and outstanding foreign plays inhibited the Polish writers and without original Polish plays the theatre could not flourish and evolve creatively. The unfortunate Festival of Contemporary

Polish Plays had compromised Polish drama in the early fifties. Now that it began to gain credit again in the eyes of the public, it could not stand up to the competition of the best foreign plays.

The only alternative that could be taken was a new reading of the great Polish classics and interpretations with the help of modern means of expressions the Polish theatre had acquired in the course of the late fifties and the sixties, as well as support to contemporary plays, whose numbers grew with each passing year.

The year 1962 may be recognized as the turning point. The decisive factor was Kazimierz Dejmek's assumption of the post of director of the *Narodowy* Theatre of Warsaw. The date also marks the beginning of the fourth period in the development of the theatre in People's Poland. Dejmek's primary objective was the conscious development of a national repertory. Reverting to the tradition established by Bogusławski, he wished this to be a *Narodowy* (National) Theatre not only in name. He resolved to put together a basic repertory representing the leading masterpieces of Polish literature, ranging from the early Polish drama, through the literature of the Enlightenment, the Polish Romantic and Neo-Romantic plays and to 20th century and contemporary drama. In the six years that he remained director of the theatre, he managed to put into effect only a part of his plans. The *Narodowy* Theatre presented *The History of the Lord's Glorious Resurrection* and *The Life of Joseph, Kordian* and *Forefathers' Eve* as well as Rittner's *Wilki w nocy* (The Wolves in the Night) and Bruno Jasieński's *Słowo o Jakubie Szeli* (A Word About Jakub Szela). For the first time in the history of the Polish theatre the following plays by Stanisław Ignacy Witkiewicz were presented on the stage: *Kurka wodna* (The Water Hen), *Mątwa* (The Cuttlefish) and *Jan Karol Maciej Wścieklica*. Adam Hanuszkiewicz launched his programme of the Polish poetic theatre at the *Powszechny* Theatre nearly at the same time as Dejmek. He produced, among others, Wyspiański's *The Wedding* and *Liberation* and Słowacki's *Kordian*. When he moved into the *Narodowy* Theatre after Dejmek, he started out by repeating these productions there. He next directed *Undivine Comedy* and *Beniowski*. Neither Dejmek nor Hanuszkiewicz ignored contemporary Polish plays. But both set very high standards because they wished to present nothing but the best works of the best writers and poets. Dejmek introduced at the *Narodowy* Theatre *Wyszedł z domu* (He Left Home) by Tadeusz Różewicz while Hanuszkiewicz directed Ernest Bryll's *Rzecz listopadowa* (Regarding November).

Dejmek and Hanuszkiewicz were not alone in the effort to add new life to the Polish poetic theatre. Konrad Swinarski working in Cracov put his efforts toward the same ends. Trained at Brecht's theatre he set out to put into effect in the interpretation of the masterpieces of the epic drama written by Polish Romantic and Neo-Romantic poets the means of expression borrowed from the arsenal of the Berliner Ensemble. The effects were sensational. The first play in the series produced at the *Stary* Theatre of Cracov was Zygmunt Krasiński's *Undivine Comedy*. The interpretation came as a surprise both to the proponents and to the opponents of the play. Swinarski made use of the technique of alienation he had learned at Brecht's school. He thus gained a critical perspective of the text and action of the play. Thanks to this method, the viewer was able to take a critical view of some of the issues. In the case of the *Undivine Comedy,* the viewer's attention was concentrated on the most essential problem, that is, a class view of the conflict between the aristocracy and the revolutionized people.

> The play tells of the fate of Count Henryk, a poet. To some degree, he is the author's *porte parole.* The first part of the play is concerned with the personal fate of the count, the second deals with civil issues. The aristocracy, threatened by the revolution, makes its last stand in the Holy Trinity trenches. The Count realizes that the aristocratic camp is doomed but he is honour bound to defend himself. The revolutionary leader Pankracy thinks very highly of Count Henryk and tries to win him over to the side of the revolution. He promises life and freedom in turn for neutrality. The dialogue between the two is one of the finest scenes of the play. The Count refuses to cooperate, preferring to fight and die. The people win a victory. Pankracy orders a search for Count Henryk and finds only his body. At the peak of fame, the revolutionary leader Pankracy dies of a heart attack. His pupil Leonard, possessed by a fanatic desire for power, assumes power after the dead leader.

Without changing Krasiński's text or altering the order of the scenes Swinarski gave an original and contemporary stage interpretation of the work bold, vibrant, interesting and thought out to the final outcome. *The Undivine Comedy* was followed by Słowacki's *Fantazy.* The director emphasized the social and realistic substance of the romantic comedy. The production was not only cutting in its humour but also shorn of the bombast of Romantic posturings. Swinarski, being in total accord with Słowacki, ridicules the different attitudes. The production of Wyspiański's two tragedies: *Sędziowie* (The Judges) and *Klątwa* (The Curse) were also exciting, discovering new meanings in the plays. They had always been played in the manner of classical tragedies concerned with implacable destiny. Swinarski interpreted them as realistic plays about life in the villages of Polish Galicia at the end of the 19th century, hence plays concerned with the ignorance and superstition of the villages and the cupidity of the Jewish innkeeper and his son *(The Judges)*, of the hypocrisy of the village priest who wishes to make a career but is frustrated by the scandal that breaks out around his housekeeper, with whom he lives as man and wife and by whom he has children *(The Curse)*. Earlier directors were prompted by the fact that the plays are poetic in character. Swinarski realized that poetry does not deny truth. On the contrary, poetry makes it possible to isolate truth. It forces the viewer to look upon the course of events, with poetic quotation marks about them, from a certain perspective. He is thus able to think critically about the issue without identifying with it and without being hypnotized by the evocative magic of the stage.

Even Jerzy Grotowski, founder of the Laboratory Theatre, willingly conducts his artistic experiments on the plays of the Polish Romantic poets. He has directed Słowacki's *Kordian* and *Forefathers' Eve* by Mickiewicz. With the help of stage designer Józef Szajna, he has constructed a modern metaphor of the Auschwitz concentration camp on the basis of Wyspiański's *Acropolis*, and created the world famous production about the suffering of man by taking Słowacki's poetic adaptation of Calderon's *The Constant Prince*.

The young generation of stage directors, who made a successful start in their careers in the late sixties, also evince a lively interest in Romantic and Neo-Romantic drama. The most talented of these Maciej Prus directed Wyspiański's *Liberation* at the Kalisz theatre in 1970, Jerzy Żuławski's *Eros and Psyche* in Szczecin and Ibsen's *Peer Gynt* in Warsaw. A gifted painter and stage director Jerzy Grzegorzewski has staged in recent years in Łódź and provided stage designs for Krasiński's *Irydion* and Wyspiański's *The Wedding*. Roman Kordziński, perhaps the least stable of the three but with a mind teeming with unusual ideas, has given a most unusual production of Słowacki's *Sen Srebrny Salomei* (Salome's Silver Dream) at the Koszalin theatre, filtering the text of the Polish romantic poet through Artaud's theatre of cruelty.

With the steadily growing interest in Polish classics and works of Polish writers who lived closer to our times, the unexplored areas in the history of Polish drama began to disappear. Apart from early Polish Enlightenment, Romantic and Neo-Romantic drama, the theatres began to produce the works of obscure poets of all ages. A recent discovery was the work of Cyprian Kamil Norwid, who died in poverty in Paris in the second half of the 19th century. He wrote of himself: "the son will overlook the writing, the grandson will read it." And so it was. Thanks to the fine production called *Norwid* at the *Narodowy* Theatre and an ably done staging of Norwid's play *Za kulisami* (Behind the Scenes), directed by Kazimierz Braun at the Słowacki Theatre of Cracow, the author has become not only a great but also a live and pertinent artist in the eyes of the present generation of Poles. Another notable Polish poet, Tadeusz Miciński, has come into his own thanks to Stanisław Hebanowski and Marek Okopiński. Miciński's work is a link between the works of Wyspiański and Witkiewicz. In 1963 Marek Okopiński directed in Poznań his *Bazilissa Teofanu* while the *Termopile polskie* (The Polish Thermopylae) received its first performance in Gdańsk in 1970. In view of the fact that the plays were written about 60 years ago and were never produced before (the author died over 50 years ago), it must be admitted that their rediscovery is indeed of great service to the Polish theatre.

Witkiewicz has an established position in the Polish theatre. His plays are being produced at many theatres although they are not always fully comprehended. In 1970, Erwin Axer directed *Mother* at the *Współczesny* Theatre, with Halina Mikołajska in the title role. It is expected that in the seventies the Polish theatre will come forth with a number of interesting productions of the works of this great dramatist, who had fallen into obscurity for so many years. Similarly, it might be expected that Witold Gombrowicz, the next in the series of great Polish dramatists, will enjoy a revival. In 1957 the *Dramatyczny* Theatre of Warsaw produced his *Iwona księżniczka Burgunda* (Ivona, Princess of Burgundy), a few years later Jerzy Jarocki and the Gliwice student theatre group put on his *Ślub* (The Marriage).

What about modern drama? The precursor of the new development in drama was Leon Kruczkowski. At the close of the fifties and in the early sixties he wrote two plays, both far ahead of their times in substance and structure. These were: *Pierwszy dzień wolności* (The First Day of Freedom), at the *Współczesny* Theatre of Warsaw directed by Erwin Axer with Tadeusz Łomnicki and Aleksandra Śląska in the leading roles and *Śmierć gubernatora* (Death of the Governor) directed by Kazimierz Dejmek at the *Polski* Theatre of Warsaw and given an excellent production by Jerzy Jarocki at the Wyspiański Theatre of Katowice, with Jerzy Kaliszewski in the lead. The painful problem of the "frightening insides of power" taken up by *Death of the Governor*, was to find its tragic solution ten years later. With the sensitive intuition of an artist Kruczkowski foresaw the course of events at the beginning of that decade. He had made sketches of two plays which he did not live to write. He died in 1962. From the plays he had written it is evident that he was headed in the direction of the epic drama filled with deep moral, philosophical and political reflections.

Kruczkowski's plays were the first to break the supremacy of foreign plays in the Polish theatre. *The First Day of Freedom* was the most popular play in the Polish theatres, competing successfully with foreign dramas. Kruczkowski's plays were followed by the brilliant works of Sławomir Mrożek. His very first plays *Policjanci* (The Police) and *Indyk* (The Turkey), both seen at the *Dramatyczny* Theatre, and his one act plays *Karol, Strip-Tease, Na pełnym morzu* (On the Open Sea) and *Zabawa* (Having a Wonderful Time) and others presaged a dramatist of the highest calibre. He clearly reverted to the style of Witkiewicz and Gombrowicz. But none of his early plays won such wide acclaim as *Tango*. It became the biggest event in the Polish theatre in the mid sixties. In Warsaw, the play received an admirable production at the hands of Erwin Axer at the *Współczesny* Theatre (Axer later directed the play at Düsseldorf) and in Cracow, Jerzy Jarocki directed the play at the *Stary* Theatre. *Tango* was produced by many Polish theatres and later by many theatres of other countries. Mrożek's success was meteoric but brief. *Tango* was not followed by anything that could equal it. Meanwhile, Polish theatres were waiting for new contemporary plays.

The late sixties brought a clear change in that area. Polish poets went back to the sources of Polish literature to seek inspiration for new ideas to their original works. The poetic play marks the dominating trend in works for the stage written in Poland today. It accords with the character and specific nature of Polish dramatic literature. The new plays take up the major issues of our world and Poland. They contemplate the fate of man and view his shortcomings and weakness with irony. Most of the plays are tragifarces, scripts that have practically no action and no stage characters in the traditional sense of the word but which give a free hand to the director and the stage designer. The precursor of that trend is the leading Polish poet Tadeusz Różewicz. He made his debut in the drama with *Kartoteka* (Personal File), staged at the *Dramatyczny* Theatre in 1960. His later plays are *Grupa Laokoona* (The Laocoön Group) and *Spaghetti i miecz* (Spaghetti and the Sword), both at the *Dramatyczny* Theatre, *Wyszedł z domu* (He Left Home), *Nasza mała stabilizacja* (Our Small Stability), *Akt przerywany* (The Interrupted Act), *Śmieszny staruszek* (The Funny Old Man) and *Stara kobieta wysiaduje* (The Old Lady Sitting). The last of these brought him wide renown thanks to the direction of Jerzy Jarocki at the *Współczesny* Theatre of Wrocław. Jarocki has a deep empathy with Różewicz and his works, as witness the excellent staging of *Moja córeczka* (My Little Daughter) at the *Stary* Theatre of Cracow, an adaptation of a film novel by Różewicz. But there are others who understand Różewicz today. Other directors have been able to strike the right chord in their readings of Różewicz's plays. Kazimierz Braun has done a very fine production of *The Interrupted Act* in Lublin and Helmut Kajzar directed *The Funny Old Man* at the *Kameralny* Theatre of Wrocław. Konrad Swinarski's interpretation of *Personal File* and *Our Small Stability* for millions of televison theatre viewers was received with applause.

The poetic plays of Ernest Bryll are winning a wide following. In the course of two short years, Bryll has completed five plays. All had a successful run in the Polish theatres. The first was *Rzecz listopadowa* (Regarding November); it was played at a number of theatres. Then came the nativity play *Po górach, po chmurach...* (Over Hills, Over Clouds...) at the *Współczesny* Theatre of Warsaw directed by Erwin Axer and at a few other theatres. It was followed by *Kurdesz* at the *Ateneum* Theatre of Warsaw directed by Janusz Warmiński and a mountain folk spectacle about the Tatra brigand Janosik, called *Na szkle malowane* (Painted on Glass), with productions in Wrocław, Łódź, Cracow and Warsaw, and finally *Kto ty jesteś* (Who Are You?), a fascinating play that takes a bitter view of contemporary issues, directed by Kazimierz Braun at the Osterwa Theatre of Lublin.

Worthy of note are the plays of the poet Stanisław Grochowiak, whose *Chłopcy* (Boys), set in a home for aged men, has been highly successful. Jerzy Przeździecki and Aleksander Ścibor-Rylski excel in plays that deal with the modern ethic.

Authors of the young generation had success with their plays in 1970. Notable among them is Jarosław Marek Rymkiewicz, author of poetic translations of Calderon which he calls imitations. His play *Król Mięsopust* (King Mardi Gras) represents a sure and deft handling of Spanish baroque poetry. The pastiche on a play performed at the court of Philip, the king of Spain, is at the same time theatre within a theatre, a device which owes a good deal to his experience in the student theatres. The play was seen at the *Stary* Theatre of Cracow, the Horzyca Theatre of Toruń and the *Narodowy* Theatre of Łódź. Helmut Kajzar, poet and director, has made a very promising beginning with a play called *Paternoster* (A Talking to), a reconstruction of a dream. The play was directed at the *Współczesny* Theatre of Wrocław by Jerzy Jarocki. The *Stary* Theatre of Cracow presented an interesting play by Tomasz Łubieński, called *Zegary* (Clocks), with an interesting concept of time and its relative values. Among authors closely connected with the theatre is Maciej Zenon Bordowicz, actor and director, whose play *Non-Stop* was staged at the *Kameralny* Theatre of Warsaw.

A growing number of theatres is becoming aware of their duty to contemporary Polish drama. Some of them, such as the *Kameralny* Theatre of Warsaw, give over all their time and effort to the production of modern Polish plays on their studio stages. For years now the *Ateneum* Theatre of Warsaw has been holding contests for first plays. The award provides not only for money (the sum is not large), but also for a production of the prize winning play by that theatre. In 1970, the management of the *Ateneum* Theatre announced that it is setting up a Drama Studio which will enable talented but inexperienced authors, who lack theatrical technique, to smooth out the kinks in the more promising works entered in the Contest. The latest new play presented at the *Ateneum* was by Feliks Falek *Wnyki* (Snares), a prize winning play in the Contest for First Plays. The *Polski* Theatre of Bydgoszcz has organized a contest for contemporary plays.

The year 1970 marks the end of twenty-five years of postwar activity in the Polish theatre. The theatre of People's Poland has developed its own style and image. It is a poetic theatre, actively involved in the affairs of the country, full of colour and action, contemplative, ironic, critical of the Polish reality and of the world. Although the theatre cherishes national tradition and often presents the works of old and new Polish writers, it does not shun the masterpieces of world drama. The repertory ranges from Aeschylus, Sophocles, Euripides and Aristophanes, through Shakespeare and Molière, Calderon and Lope de Vega, Goethe and Schiller and to Gorky, Mayakovsky, Brecht and contemporary writers. It is an open theatre, ready to accept new trends in art, but at the same time eager to share its experience with the world.

Has the Polish theatre said everything? In the new circumstances, it will probably wish to enter energetically into the national debate on the present and future of the country which had started at the turn of the seventies.

CHAPTER IV

STAGE DIRECTORS

The 19th century theatre was noted for its great actors. The era of the *Rozmaitości* Theatre of Warsaw, the best and most famous 19th century theatre in Poland, was the era of stars. People went to the theatre to see actors and not for the plays or the stage direction. The situation did not change but for some small minor details throughout the twenty interwar years even though great directors, such as Leon Schiller, Juliusz Osterwa, Aleksander Węgierko, Edmund Wierciński, Karol Borowski, Stanisława Perzanowska and several others, were already active in Poland at the time and although their role grew in importance. But these exceptions may be said to prove the validity of the rule.

Stage directors finally gained a major say in People's Poland. It is they who became the ideologues of the new theatre who gave it direction, shape and form, it is they who are responsible for the most important artistic developments. They have now risen to pre-eminence over the actors and the stage designers. The statement might be made that the theatre of People's Poland was the theatre of stage directors in the first twenty-five year period of its existence.

Leon Schiller set the tone in the early postwar years. This great director, whose theatre was derived from the vision of Wyspiański and the dreams of Mickiewicz, had enough strength and energy to build a bridge between the old and the new times. His political views, developed in the period between the two world wars, gave him the moral right to set up a theatre based on principles that coincided with the ideas of Socialist art in People's Poland. He was an advocate of spectacular opulence, of a theatre which merged poetic language with picture and music. His theatre was much like what we today call the total theatre.

Bronisław Dąbrowski also represented the monumental epic theatre. Sensitive to pictures, hues and sound, Dąbrowski's spontaneous talent found an outlet in spectacular stage shows. Working at the Słowacki Theatre in Cracow and from 1950 to 1955 at the *Polski* in Warsaw, his productions were noted for their broad sweep and dynamism. Although his style may be compared with that of Schiller, yet it is perhaps less celebral. It seems to spring from intuition, emotional inspiration and a superb sense of the theatre.

The late Wilam Horzyca combined an excellent knowledge of literature with talent as director. He also belonged to the group whose style bore a resemblance to Schiller's. Horzyca had worked many years in close collaboration with Schiller. He put less emphasis on the visual aspect of the production (though he did not neglect it), concentrating on the exposition of the text and the beauty of the spoken word. He also paid close attention to the movement and gestures of his actors.

Another outstanding stage director, whose personality was formed before the war but which found full expression in the theatre of People's Poland, was Iwo Gall. He got his training at the *Reduta* Theatre although he set out in search of a theatre on his own before the war. Iwo Gall was a painter and stage director, and so he was primarily interested in the visual side of the production although he had learned at the *Reduta* to work with the actor. He showed great concern for the actor and his development and being a gifted teacher was able to help and nudge his talent alone. In the first year after the war, Iwo Gall set up an actors' studio in Cracow which attracted a group of talented young artists. He then went to the Coast (Gdynia) to set up a theatre, taking the artists with him. The atmosphere and the principles behind Iwo Gall's studio were reminiscent of the artistic ideas behind *Reduta*. The activity of the studio gave good results. Gall's greatest single success was the first prize for the theatre at the Shakespearean Festival held in 1947. The Wybrzeże Theatre appeared in *As You Like It* directed by Iwo Gall and with his stage sets. Many of the actors trained in Gall's studio and theatre are playing an important role in the life of the theatre today. Like Horzyca, Gall was a proponent of the poetic theatre. The most memorable of his productions was Tadeusz Gajcy's *Homer and Orchid,* a posthumous tribute to the young talented poet who died during the Warsaw Uprising in 1944.

Juliusz Osterwa survived the war by only two years. Yet before he died in 1947, he had clearly staked out the line of his artistic interests. He had always occupied a position poles apart from Schiller's ideas on the theatre. Osterwa remained faithful to himself in People's Poland as well. Working at first in Łódź and later heading the Cracow theatre until his death, he subscribed to psychological and poetic realism. He was especially careful that the actors should incorporate the whole inner and external truth of the characters they portrayed. With the minute analysis of character and the

Edmund Wierciński — caricature by Artur Swinarski

attention he gave to the slightest detail of expression, he serves as the best example.

Edmund Wierciński may be placed midway between Osterwa and Schiller. He, too, is a graduate of the *Reduta* where he acquired an admiration for Polish Romantic poetry and learned the skill of working with the actor from Osterwa. Later, however, he became interested in the new trends in art, notably: Formism, Cubism, Futurism. His new interests were reflected in the concepts that went into the highly acclaimed production of Kruszewski's *Sen* (The Dream), produced at Poznań before the war and into some of the plays he directed in Lvov. He reached the top of his form in the late thirties with *Lato w Nohant* (Summer in Nohant), a play about Chopin by Jarosław Iwaszkiewicz that he directed at the *Polski* Theatre of Warsaw. After the war Wierciński was attracted by the large spectaculars. His ambition to produce a poetic stage show found an outlet. He directed *Electra* by Giraudoux at the Poetic Theatre he founded in Łódź shortly after the war and Shakespeare's *As You Like It* in Wrocław. In Warsaw, Wierciński directed a series of large scale poetic spectacles for the *Polski* Theatre, first of these was Corneille's *Le Cid*. There was also the beautifully composed production of Słowacki's *Horsztyński* as transcribed by Wyspiański, with Karol Adwentowicz in the title role, and finally the lyrical and brilliantly colourful production of Musset's *Lorenzaccio*. Wierciński was extremely thorough and precise in his work both when he polished the actor's delivery and gesture and when he composed the picture on the stage. He tended to be too fastidious in his esthetic tastes, too finicky, so that in the end the picture on stage struck one as almost too beautiful, too smooth.

A number of other stage directors who had made a name for themselves before the war continued also in People's Poland. These included: Karol Borowski (one of the leading stage directors of Szyfman's theatre), Władysław Krasnowiecki, Henryk Szletyński (theatre director in Wrocław, Cracow and Warsaw), Hugon Moryciński (director of the Łódź theatres before the war), Stanisława Perzanowska (principal stage director of the Jaracz theatre), Aleksander Rodziewicz (before the war director of the *Ziemia Wołyńska* Theatre) and others.

Two eminent artists of the theatre known before the war made their mark in the Polish theatre only after the war. The first of these was Bohdan Korzeniewski, who before the war devoted himself to criticism and theatre history. After the war he was first appointed literary director of a Łódź theatre where he later tried his powers as a stage director with notable success. He made his debut as a stage director cooperating with the fine actor Jacek Woszczerowicz who appeared in nearly all the plays he directed. Korzeniewski was fascinated with French culture, the clarity of thought and logic and the French writers' skill in dramatic construction. He also proved a perceptive interpreter of the best works of Russian literature, especially the satires. He selected the Polish plays he wished to direct with great care, seeing to it that they accorded with his literary and intellectual interest. Korzeniewski's strength lay in the analysis of the text and in his ability to heighten the impact by raising the temperature of the conflict, by creating, sharp and drastic situations and by the expressive acting he demanded of his actors. Great epic spectacles were alien to Korzeniewski's style. He was not good in crowd scenes although there was a period when he tackled plays that called for this ability. Korzeniewski scored his biggest success in the intimate dramas. Perhaps no other stage director in the Polish theatre could equal him when it came to exposing the pettiness, hypocrisy and worthlessness of the bourgeoisie, he viciously branded the abject sordidness of man and of the world in which he lives.

Among Korzeniewski's finest works were Molière's *L'Ecole des Femmes* and primarily *Don Juan* which he directed in Warsaw, Łódź, Cracow and for the television theatre. The Cracow production presented the summit of his interpretations of that masterpiece. He also directed *Les Fourberies de Scapin* on two separate occasions. In Russian literature, he most admired the satires, ranging from Gogol through Sukhovo-Kobylin to Mayakovsky. His *Revizor* will be long remembered, with Jan Kurnakowicz turning in a marvellous performance as the *Khorodnichy* (Bailiff). His productions of Sukhovo Kobylin's *The Trial* and *Death of Tarelkin* were astringently biting (the part of Tarelkin was superbly done by Jacek Woszczerowicz) as was his staging of Mayakovsky's *The Bath*. As regards Polish stage works, he was happiest with Fredro's comedies. His staging of *Man and Wife*, filled with subtle irony and not so subtle erotics, as well as *The Revenge*, featuring Jan Kurnakowicz as the Cup Bearer and with emphasis placed on the social sense of the work, won high critical acclaim. Among Korzeniewski's more interesting works, one must also include plays which required his adaptive skill and his acumen as authority on literature and the theatre. Korzeniewski corrected and improved old translations of plays he wished to direct or wrote new versions of these. He took great pleasure in bringing to the stage plays that were either unknown or unfinished, that is plays he could adapt to the modern stage. One of these was Stefan Żeromski's *Grzech* (The Sin), a newly discovered play at the time. It related in style to Russian plays and accorded with the rules of critical realism. Another was the play of the Lithuanian writer Baltushis called *The Cocks Crow* and finally Isaak Babel's *Zmierzch* (Dusk). Korzeniewski served as director of the *Narodowy* Theatre for a few years. During that period he directed, among others, Nikolai Pogodin's *Man with a Gun,* with Jacek Woszczerowicz playing Lenin and Jan Kurnakowicz as the Russian peasant Shadrin. The two great stage artists were Korzeniewski's favourite interpreters in the plays he directed.

Another interesting stage director to emerge in the Polish theatre was Jakub Rotbaum. He had established his position as director before the war. After the war he directed at the State Jewish Theatre. One of his most brilliant productions was the musical called *A Dream About Goldfaden.* In the fifties Rotbaum put his talents to the test in the Polish language theatre, scoring a notable success in Wrocław. For a number of years Rotbaum served as art director of the Wrocław theatres without severing his ties with the Jewish theatre. In personality and interest he came closer to Schiller than Korzeniewski. Being a painter, Rotbaum had a deep sense of stage composition. He liked spectaculars and crowd scenes which he did most effectively. On the other hand, he also liked plays of critical realism and during his stay in the Soviet Union gained a wide knowledge of Russian literature and of the specific atmosphere of that country. Nor was he ignorant of the expressionistic trends of the German theatre and literature for they exercised a certain influence on the Jewish theatre in Poland in the interwar period. He also knew and thought highly of the work of Bertolt Brecht.

77

Among Rotbaum's best productions, directed at Wrocław, was *The Wedding,* in which he remained faithful to Wyspiański's concept, the adaptation of Julian Stryjkowski's novel *Bieg do Fragala* (Race to Fragala) and the staging of Aleksander Ostrovsky's *And a Horse Stumbles* as well as of Pogodin's *Man with a Gun.* Other notable Rotbaum productions were a play about Julius Fučik, the hero of the Czech resistance movement and a striking presentation of Brecht's *The Threepenny Opera* and *The Resistible Rise of Arturo Ui.*

We might now turn our attention to the works of directors who made their first steps in the theatre just before the outbreak of war and who did their best work in People's Poland and to directors who began to work and to develop their talents after the war. These fall into three groups: the first entered the theatre directly after the war, the second made their debuts in the fifties and the third youngest group began work in the sixties. The first two groups were under the influence of Leon Schiller, the third was trained by Schiller's successors, specifically by Bohdan Korzeniewski, for many long years dean of the department of stage directing at the State Theatre School of Warsaw.

Schiller had founded a department of stage directing at the State Institute of Theatre Art in Warsaw before the war. This was the first modern school offering training to stage directors in Europe. After the war Schiller continued the work he had begun at the State Theatre School in Łódź and later in Warsaw. Among Schiller's students during the prewar period were: Erwin Axer, Aleksander Bardini and Józef Wyszomirski. The following now famous stage directors are graduates of his schools: Ludwik René, Lidia Zamkow, Krystyna Skuszanka, Jerzy Krasowski and Kazimierz Dejmek.

Though Dejmek did not study long with Schiller, yet he represented his ideas of the theatre most closely. It is a tribute to the pedagogical talent of Schiller and to his attitude to his pupils that not one of them seeks to imitate the master. Some, like Erwin Axer, have taken the opposite view of the art of the theatre, others have followed the path blazed by him but placed the stamp of their own personality on the work they do.

In the fifties the group of Polish directors was enlarged by such forceful personalities as Jerzy Grotowski (who studied directing at Moscow), Konrad Swinarski (who honed his talents under the tutelage of Bertold Brecht in Berlin), Adam Hanuszkiewicz (an actor, whose first success as director came in television where he served as head director of the television theatre, followed by other successes in the theatre), Jerzy Kreczmar (for many years literary director of Axer's theatre, he made his debut after the war as director of avant-garde and intimate dramas, a field in which he has done remarkable work), Jan Maciejowski (for many years managing director of the Szczecin theatres), Andrzej Witkowski (director of the *Współczesny* Theatre of Wrocław), Jerzy Jarocki (graduate of the Leningrad theatre school, best noted for his staging of Polish contemporary plays), Marek Okopiński (for many years director of the theatres of Zielona Góra, Poznań and Gdańsk), Józef Gruda (director of the Szczecin theatres), Jerzy Goliński, Zygmunt Hübner, Kazimierz Braun, Irena Babel, Jerzy Zagalski, and others. A group of young talented directors reinforced the existing number in the early sixties. They are: Jan Błeszyński (director of the theatre of Olsztyn), Andrzej Ziębiński (director of the Poznań theatres), Krystyna Tyszarska (director of the Gorzów theatre), Teresa Żukowska, Krystyna Meissner.

Izabella Cywińska (director of the Kalisz theatre).

Henryk Tomaszewski, the founder of the Pantomime Theatre of Wrocław, represents a unique phenomenon in the life of the Polish theatre. Tomaszewski has contributed new values to the dramatic theatre. In the sixties he became interested in collaboration with the dramatic theatre. The result was the highly original staging of *Marat/Sade* by Weiss in Poznań. *Protesilas and Laodamia* by Wyspiański in Wrocław as well as Kafka's *The Trial* and Wyspiański's *The Curse* which he directed in Oslo.

The youngest generation of Polish directors are talented artists. They will have much to say in the Polish theatre in the seventies. Their interest lies clearly in the poetic theatre and in Polish Romantic and Neo-Romantic literature. It follows the general trend of the Polish theatre today. The most talented perhaps is Maciej Prus who studied with Bohdan Korzeniewski at the Theatre School and spent some time working under Grotowski. He has won considerable attention with Marlowe's *Edward II*, Ibsen's *Peer Gynt* and with Polish plays, notably Wyspiański's *Liberation,* Żuławski's *Eros and Psyche* and Stanisław Ignacy Witkiewicz's *Jan Karol Maciej Wścieklica.* Another talented young director is Jerzy Grzegorzewski who is also a stage designer. He works in Łódź where he directed, among others, Brecht's *The Caucasian Chalk Circle,* Krasiński's *Irydion* and Wyspiański's *The Wedding.* The third in the group is the highly gifted and imaginative Roman Kordziński. One may argue with his concept of *Crime and Punishment* or of *Salome's Silver Dream* by Słowacki, but one cannot deny that his is an inventive and original talent. Very talented as well is poet, dramatist and director in one person, Helmut Kajzar who

Zofia Małynicz and Janina Romanówna in
Non-Stop by Maciej Zenon Bordowicz at the
Kameralny Theatre of Warsaw

Janusz Warnecki in the television production of Zdzisław Skowroński's *Maestro*

Tadeusz Łomnicki and Barbara Krafftówna in Dürrenmatt's *Play Strindberg* at the *Współczesny* Theatre of Warsaw. Direction and stage design by Andrzej Wajda

Purple Dust by Sean O'Casey, directed and produced by Józef Szajna at the Stanisław Wyspiański Theatre of Silesia in Katowice

Halina Mikołajska in the title role of Mother by Stanisław Ignacy Witkiewicz directed by Erwin Axer, with stage sets by Ewa
Starowieyska, at the *Współczesny* Theatre of Warsaw

Halina Mikołajska and Jan Świderski in Ionesco's *The Chairs* directed by Ludwik René, with stage sets by Jan Kosiński, at the *Dramatyczny* Theatre of Warsaw

Revizor by Gogol at the *Ludowy* Theatre of Nowa Huta directed and with stage sets by Józef Szajna

Leon Kruczkowski's *The First Day of Freedom* at the *Polski* Theatre of Wrocław. Ferdynand Matysiak, Witold Hrydzewicz and Witold Pyrkosz.

De Ghelderode's *La Ballades du Grande Macabre* directed by Jerzy Krasowski with stage sets by Krystyna Zachwatowicz at the *Kameralny* Theatre of Wrocław

Every summer musical shows are put on at the Theatre on the Island in Łazienki Park in Warsaw. Scene from an 18th century opera *Apollo the Lawgiver*, directed by Jan Kulma, with musical adaptation by Stefan Sutkowski

Elżbieta Kępińska and Anna Seniuk in Genet's *The Maids* at the *Ateneum* Theatre of Warsaw

Roman Kordziński represents the new generation of Polish stage directors. Scene from Słowacki's *Salome's Silver Dream* directed by Kordziński at the *Bałtycki* Theatre of Koszalin

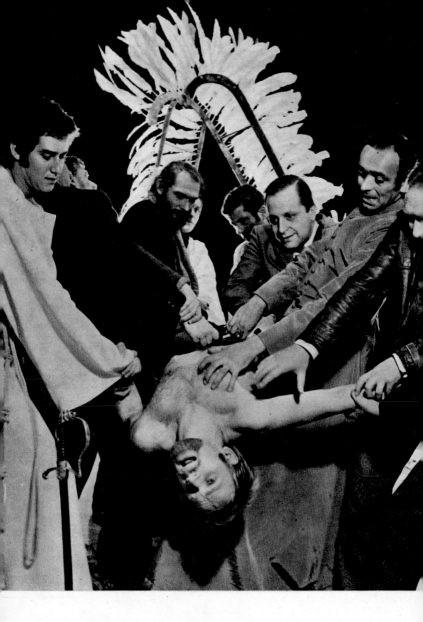

Crowd scene from Wyspiański's *Liberation*, directed by Maciej Prus

has directed *Oedipus Rex* and the plays of Tadeusz Różewicz. Maciej Zenon Bordowicz, another poet, director
and dramatist, has had his greatest success as director
with Shakespeare's *Henry V* at the *Powszechny* Theatre
of Łódź. The group also includes: Cracow theorist on
the theatre, essayist and pedagogue Bohdan Hussakow-
ski, the talented organizer of the whole group Piotr
Piaskowski and finally Wojciech Boratyński. It might
be pointed out that some of the directors came to the
schools of the theatre from the student theatres and
that a number of them still maintain a lively contact
with them. Izabella Cywińska decided to establish a kind
of "nursery school" in Kalisz where young directors
can experiment with ideas in staging. Maciej Prus and
Helmut Kajzar direct at the Kalisz theatre.

It is evident from the brief list of names that the
Polish theatre has at its service a richly diversified
group of directors with distinct creative individualities.
What are the main art trends and currents that Polish
directors, irrespective of age and generation, subscribe
to from their debut and through the years of work in
the theatre?

It is possible to distinguish a number of trends in the
Polish theatre represented by its leading directors. The
most pronounced of these, which defines to a considerable degree the style of the contemporary theatre in
Poland, is that of the monumental poetic theatre. The
movement reverts clearly to Polish national tradition.
The most eminent representatives of that movement
accept the principle of the spectacular theatre.

Kazimierz Dejmek, the leading proponent of that
trend, deliberately brutalizes his productions by introducing elements of folk and plebeian culture and art.
His method is most clearly in evidence in the early

Polish dramas staged by him. Hanuszkiewicz, on the other hand, introduces into his stage productions the visual composition technique of the television theatre and other techniques borrowed from the arsenal of the Eleventh Muse. Thus, the masterpieces are updated and rejuvenated in a new original visual form. These tendencies were evident in his productions of Wyspiański's *The Wedding* and *Liberation* and principally in *Crime and Punishment*. Hanuszkiewicz took a most original and creative approach to the staging of *Danton's Death* by Büchner, making use of montage, stage synthesis, flashes, jazz and other attributes of the modern theatre, manipulating the lights to give the effect of a television camera. The new epic theatre, structured on the foundation of Romantic poetry and the work of those who continued its tradition, finds its fullest expression in Hanuszkiewicz's staging of *Norwid* and *Beniowski*. Both are totally deprived of action although the characters are sharply delineated and the text, modelled with great artistry and buttressed by the machinery of the theatre, comes through each time as a virtuoso concert of solo voices. The theatre of Hanuszkiewicz, like Schiller's and Dejmek's theatre, is opulent. It relies not only on the spoken text, but also on the play of colour, light, stage and costume effects, music, movement, dance and pantomime.

A whole group of Polish directors takes part in search for this kind of theatre, though each has his individual vision of it. Henryk Tomaszewski, past master of pantomime and stage movement, may be included among their number as may be Lidia Zamkow who, with her astringent and aggressive composition of situations on the stage, shows a weakness for the expressionistic theatre (*Caligula* by Camus, *Uncle's*

Dream by Dostoievsky, *Mother Courage, The Three-Penny Opera* and *A Man's a Man* by Brecht, Gorky's *The Lower Depths* and *Barbarians* and Vishnevsky's *An Optimistic Tragedy*), Ludwik René who composes very attractive stage scenes in close and long cooperation with Jan Kosiński (Wyspiański's *Royal Chronicles,* Brecht's *The Good Woman of Setzuan* and *Schweik in the Second World War* and Dürrenmatt's *The Visit*). Like Schiller, René is attracted by the lyric theatre and directs operas from time to time. After his early successes in the dramatic theatre, Aleksander Bardini now devotes his time almost exclusively to the opera where he has been directing over the past years.

Krystyna Skuszanka and Jerzy Krasowski hold a leading position among the representatives of the Polish poetic and monumental theatre. For a number of years they directed the *Ludowy* Theatre of Nowa Huta. At present, they have been directing the Wrocław theatres since 1966. Skuszanka and Krasowski's programatic production at the Nowa Huta Theatre was Goldoni's *Servant of Two Masters* which clearly reverts to the brilliant stylization, frothy humour and expressiveness of the Vakhtangov theatre. Skuszanka and Krasowski's admiration of the poetic stage epic manifested itself in the lovely production of *Forefathers' Eve* at Nowa Huta and their interest in contemporary social and political problems in their presentation of Steinbeck's *Of Mice and Men* and *Smok* (The Dragon) by Szwarc (the world première) as well as in their adaptation of Ilia Ehrenburg's novel *Leyzorek Roitschvanets* and of *Radość z odzyskanego śmietnika* (Joy at the Recovered Dump), according to the novel by Juliusz Kaden-Bandrowski. In Wrocław their search for theatre is clearly headed toward the poetic theatre as

illustrated by their productions of Słowacki's *Kordian,*
Salome's Silver Dream and *Fantazy,* Shakespeare's *As*
You Like It, The Tempest and *Measure for Measure* and
finally Fredro's *The Revenge* as well as *The Danton*
Case and *Demidor* by Stanisława Przybyszewska.

Other directors who may be included in the same
group are: Jan Maciejowski, who presented a beautifully
staged series of Shakespearean plays and Wyspiański's
Liberation in Szczecin; Jerzy Goliński, director of Słowacki's *Zawisza Czarny* (Zawisza the Black) and *Złota*
Czaszka (The Gold Skull) and Wyspiański's *The Wedding*
and *Powrót Odysa* (The Homecoming of Odysseus);
Kazimierz Braun, a director who has a special fondness
for Norwid staging his *Actor* and *Behind the Scenes,*
though he has done a very interesting production of
Hamlet, Mother Courage, The Good Woman of Setzuan
and *Caucasian Chalk Circle* by Brecht and *Interrupted*
Act by Różewicz; Jerzy Zagalski, producer of
Forefathers' Eve and *Hamlet;* Józef Gruda, director of
attractive productions of *The Wedding, The Revenge*
and *Hamlet;* Andrzej Witkowski, who has to his credit
Horsztyński, Zawisza the Black and *Zborowski* by Słowacki and Żeromski's *Rose;* Jan Błeszyński, director of
Marlowe's *Edward II;* Andrzej Ziębiński, whose staging
of *The Cracovians and the Mountaineers* was
remarkable for its movement and colour; Irena Babel,
who directed *Kordian, Rose* and *the Caucasian Chalk*
Circle. The young directors who are taking the same
line in the theatre are: Maciej Prus, Jerzy Grzegorzewski
and Roman Kordziński.

At the opposite pole to the "opulent theatre" is the
"poor theatre" founded by Jerzy Grotowski, authority
in the stage arts. He has rejected everything; stage
sets, costumes, lighting, music, even the stage itself. He

promulgates the programme of an ascetic theatre where the actor and his body is the only material to work with. All he requires is an empty hall where he places his actors and a small handful of spectators (34 at the most) to create the most extraordinary kind of spectacle that recalls something on the order of a medieval mystery play, black mass ritual and processions of flagellants. However, Grotowski does not attach much importance to religious substance. He places stress on theatre ritual and on its sacral forms which, true enough, have been developed over the centuries in connection with religious ceremony. Realizing that religious and secular myth is deeply imbedded in the human psyche, he wishes to resuscitate these archetypes and to confront them with problems that beset modern man. Grotowski considers himself a continuator of the Stanislavsky method. He elaborates and intensifies the original Stanislavsky concept by beginning his search of theatre at the point wher the founder of the Moscow Art Theatre ended his, that is, from the theory of physical action enhanced by the biomechanics of Meyerhold. In perfecting acting technique, the physical and vocal flexibility of the actor, he borrows heavily from the theatres of Asia: the Peking opera, the Hindu Kathakali and the Japanese No theatre. Yet he remains faithful to the Polish theatre tradition, recognizing as his forerunner Juliusz Osterwa, founder of *Reduta* who adapted to the Polish theatre and gave a Polish form to the Stanislavsky method. There are many similarities between the principles adopted by Grotowski's Laboratory Theatre and the principles embraced by *Reduta*. These are: ensemble work, deliberate and voluntary rejection of material goods, a style and way of life reminiscent of a sect or religious order and an attempt to draw the spectators into an active participation with the actors in the spectacle. In the beginning Grotowski attached great importance to this last principle. However, he has since come to the realization that an active attitude on the part of the spectators is not possible in the theatre and assigns to them the role of witnesses subjected to the intensive influence of the actors.

Grotowski does not accord much importance to the literary text, he is arbitrary about changes and cuts in the plays. To him the play provides the myths which serve as material to work on. The more widely known a literary work, the more deeply rooted in the consciousness of the people is the myth that lies at its basis. That explains why he relies on the masterpieces of Polish and world literature in his theatre, both in Opole where he began his activity in 1959 and in Wrocław where he has been working since 1965. The Bible, and more strictly speaking the New Testament, also provides the plots on which he bases his production, witness the latest *Apocalypsis cum figuris*. Here, Grotowski confronts the Christ myth, specifically the Passion, with the situation, alienation and anguish of contemporary man. The effect is shattering. The Grotowski theatre is a cruel theatre, although it is not a theatre of cruelty, for he strives to depict the real fears and obsessions that afflict modern man. In his theatre, the integration between actors and the spectators is nearly complete.

Konrad Swinarski takes a totally different approach. He subscribes to a theatre that employs a wide variety of artistic expression. Swinarski has a painter's imagination and shows a preference for striking stage sets and ostentatious costume. He places emphasis on movement and gesture and gladly introduces music into his productions. But he uses the whole gamut of measures and techniques of the opulent theatre in order to underline the theatricality of the spectacle, to shatter the deceptive illusion of reality, to stress that the action is taking place in the theatre and only in the theatre. These are factors that help the spectator alienate himself and gain a perspective on the actions transpiring on the stage, inducing or even compelling him to assume a critical position toward the things taking place on stage. Thus, Swinarski's theatre teaches critical thinking and breaks with clichés and the deeply rooted patterns of thought. It is abundantly clear from his productions that Swinarski is the product of Brecht's school.

The Polish intimate literary theatre stands halfway between the opulent and the poor theatre, between the emotional theatre and the theatre of critical thinking. The most celebrated proponent of that theatre is Erwin Axer and his *Współczesny* Theatre. For the past twenty years the theatre has been identified with productions prepared with great care and taste. Erwin Axer places emphasis on the literary qualities of the text. He is an unrivalled master of stage direction and dialogue interpretations capable of extracting the maximum of substance and expression from the text. With his fine group of actors, he has the necessary tools for the realization of this programme. His is a thoughtful and a sceptical theatre, lost deep in a contemplation of the destiny of man, raising questions to which he does not in fact supply an answer. Like its name, this is above all a theatre devoted to a contemporary repertory.

Erwin Axer has made a sizeable contribution in his time. He has directed a number of outstanding contemporary plays by Polish and other writers. His theatre

87

gave the first production of *The Germans* and *Pierwszy dzień wolności* (The First Day of Freedom) by Kruczkowski, the first production of Mrożek's *Tango*, the first Polish production of Brecht's *The Resistible Rise of Arturo Ui* and *The Firebugs* by Frisch. Erwin Axer also directed *Mother* by Stanisław Ignacy Witkiewicz with a complete awareness of the relevance of that great play to our times. He had occasionally gone back to the classics whenever he discovered points of correspondence with the problems of our day. Thus, he gave us interpretations of Chekhov's *Three Sisters*, Schiller's *Mary Stuart* and finally *Iphigenie auf Tauris* by Goethe in a new translation by Edward Csato. The last production attracted wide popular interest. Axer does not subscribe to any of the avant-garde movements. He professes the ideas of a moderately modern theatre of realism in an updated form, known in Poland also as the Neo-realistic theatre. This theatre is concerned with problems of current ethics and philosophy and with the social and political issues of our times. He places the main emphasis on truth in dialogue, stage action and character development without probing into the psychological motifs but with considerable attention to the esthetics and composition of the action on stage.

Axer's tastes are supplemented ably at the *Współczesny* Theatre by the direction of Jerzy Kreczmar. Kreczmar subscribes to the ideas of the Paris avant-garde movement of the fifties and the early sixties, to the theatre of the absurd of which he is perhaps the best authority in Poland in theory and practice. The first performance in Poland of Beckett's *Waiting for Godot* was given at the *Współczesny* Theatre on January 21st, 1957. The play was directed by Kreczmar as were *Exit the King* by Ionesco, Pinter's *The Birthday Party* and

Stanisława Perzanowska in *He Who Laughs Last Laughs Loudest*
— caricature by Adam Perzyk

Edward Albee's *Who's Afraid of Virginiu Woolf?* Krecz-mar was also interested in the Polish romantic drama, but did not score any noticeable success in that area. He served as director of the *Polski* Theatre of Warsaw for a number of years but in the end returned to the *Współczesny* where he has remained to this day.

Jerzy Jarocki, one of the most talented directors of the middle generation, also devotes himself to the staging of intimate drama. He concentrates his efforts on contemporary plays and, it might be said, with success. No other Polish director has displayed anything like the skill demonstrated by Jarocki in analysing and understanding the latest plays of Polish authors or in giving as lucid and clear a stage interpretation. Shortly after completing his studies, he directed at the student theatre of Gliwice *Ślub* (The Marriage) by Gombrowicz. Though working with amateurs this first production was a striking and widely acclaimed success. Then came Bruno Jasieński's *Bal manekinów* (The Mannequin Ball), *Głupiec i inni* (A Fool and Others) by Jerzy Broszkiewicz, *Portret* (The Portrait) by Jan Paweł Gawlik and most memorable perhaps Leon Kruczkowski's *Death of the Governor*. In Cracow, Jarocki directed Mrożek's *Tango*, a very interesting staging of the play, very different from the Warsaw production by Axer, some of the critics thought it the better of the two.

The works of Różewicz occupy a separate chapter in Jarocki's career. It can be stated without fear that it was Jarocki who brought down the barrier between that author's fine work and the Polish audiences. It was he who discovered the most appropriate stage form for *He Left Home* and it was he who adapted the film novel *Moja córeczka* (My Little Daughter) for the stage. But he was most successful with *Stara kobieta wysiaduje* (An Old Woman Sitting) which he directed at the *Współczesny* Theatre of Wrocław. There too Jarocki directed the play of the young director and dramatist Helmut Kajzar, called *Paternoster*. Reacting as he does to current issues, Jerzy Jarocki could not fail to turn his attention to the stage works of Mayakovsky. Among his best were *The Bath* in Katowice and *Bedbug* at Wrocław.

Bohdan Korzeniewski, who has already been discussed here, was always interested in intimate drama of literary significance. Aside from the *Współczesny,* a number of other Polish theatres put on this type of repertory. The *Ateneum* in Warsaw, headed by Janusz Warmiński, a perceptive authority on American literature and experienced in directing the plays of American dramatists (Arthur Miller, Edward Albee and others), comes closest to this ideal. The Helena Modrzejewska (Modjeska) Theatre of Cracow focuses on this type of repertory as well. For many years the theatre was headed by Władysław Krzemiński, noted for his excellent productions of Miller's *Death of a Salesman* and the plays of Tennessee Williams. He is also an authority on Russian literature and has done some of his best work in Tolstoy's *Fruits of Education* and Ostrovsky's *The Forest.* He also adapted and staged Breza's *Urząd* (The Office). His successor as theatre director was Zygmunt Hübner who has proved himself not only a remarkable art director of the *Stary* Theatre but also an interesting director. He directed *Ulysses* by Joyce at the *Wybrzeże* Theatre of Gdańsk with notable success.

The present director of the *Wybrzeże* is the talented director Marek Okopiński. The wide range of his interests encompasses the intimate drama as well. He directed The *Actor's Demise* and *Mademoiselle Jaire* by Michel de Ghelderode and the Polish poetic dramas of the period of Modernism, otherwise known as Young Poland. Among his achievements in the second category are the beautifully done production of Wyspiański's *Liberation* directed at Zielona Góra, *Bazilissa Teofanu* by Tadeusz Miciński directed in Poznań and the same author's *Termopile polskie* (The Polish Thermopylae) directed in 1970 in Gdańsk. In Poznań also Okopiński staged Leon Kruczkowski's *Kordian i cham* (Kordian and the Boor).

Wanda Laskowska is interested primarily in the Polish avant-garde drama. She directed *Personal File* by Tadeusz Różewicz at the *Dramatyczny* Theatre of Warsaw in 1960 and later devoted herself to the works of Stanisław Ignacy Witkiewicz which she directed with great sensitivity and care at the *Narodowy* and the *Ateneum*. The talented stage designer Zofia Pietrusińska has collaborated with her on this type of play for many years.

This review would be incomplete if we failed to mention the work of Polish television directors. There are among them leading Polish stage directors who find time to do work in the realm of the Eleventh Muse. Notable among these is Ludwik René, Konrad Swinarski, Bohdan Korzeniewski, Erwin Axer, Jerzy Krasowski, Janusz Warmiński, Zygmunt Hübner, Kazimierz Braun and others. Adam Hanuszkiewicz has now abandoned the television theatre for the stage, though he returns to do very attractive programmes. Jerzy Antczak began his career as director in the theatre but found full play for his energies and talent only in the television theatre. He directed the widely acclaimed television version of the *Maestro* for which he received the 1970 Grand Prix at the television festival held in Varna. He found an excellent partner in the person of Zdzisław Skowroński, the script writer. His latest television programmes included: the documentary dramatization called *Epilog norymberski* (The Nuremberg Epilogue) and *Uncle Vanya* done in Belgrade for the Yugoslav television which received the Grand Prix at the annual television festival held at Bled.

Very often we see directors who work in one branch of the performing arts making guest appearances in another branch of the art. For example, we find film directors staging plays in the theatre. One of the most successful is the famous film director Andrzej Wajda. Among his finer attempts in the theatre was the Gdańsk production of *Hamlet*, the Cracow production of *The Wedding* and the truly remarkable direction of Dürrenmatt's *Play Strindberg* in Warsaw. As artist and stage designer, Wajda quite understandably designs his own sets.

It is one of the old traditions of the Polish and world theatre that outstanding performers act as directors. In Poland we have: Jan Świderski (Rittner's *Crazy Jacob* and Dürrenmatt's *Romulus the Great*), Gustaw Holoubek (Fredro's *The Revenge* and *Mazepa* for the television theatre), Tadeusz Łomnicki, Andrzej Łapicki and others. We shall discuss their activity at length in the chapter on Polish actors.

A noteworthy development of recent years is the closer relation between directing and stage design. Andrzej Pronaszko revealed great staging talent though he modestly remained in the shadow of his director. He always came forth with suggestions which prompted or helped the director hit upon the best solution regarding the arrangement of actors on stage, and this, as we know, is an important part of the *mis en scéne*. Among contemporary Polish stage directors there are a few who have studied art and now design their own sets (Swinarski, Wajda, Grzegorzewski, and formerly Gall). We also observe a different development over the past decade. Stage designers are beginning to devote themselves to directing. The trend was initiated by Tadeusz Kantor, with experimental production in the avant-garde Cracow theatre *Cricot 2*. He later directed in the ordinary theatres. Noted Cracow stage designer and artist Józef Szajna followed in his footsteps. His interesting work may be frequently seen in the Polish theatres. The visual side outweighs all the other elements. Being an artist, Szajna thinks in pictures and pays less attention to the text and its dramatic function. But this approach to a play sometimes gives very interesting and exciting new results. This applies to the Katowice production of Bryll's *Regarding November*. It must be admitted in all fairness that Szajna's stage design played an important role in the production of *Acropolis* directed by Grotowski.

CHAPTER V

STAGE DESIGNERS

Polish stage design is influenced above all by painting. That is to say, it concerns itself not only with the purely structural function, with stage architecture or with the creation of a setting for stage action. Great weight is placed on colour and on the shapes of the stage sets as independent artistic values closely linked with the production.

The originator of the modern trend in Polish stage design was Stanisław Wyspiański. He set out to banish from the Cracow theatre the standard "outdoor areas" and the "drawing room interiors" taken from the theatre store-room, or worse still borrowed, and instead introduced original sets designed especially for his plays. The sketches for the stage sets of *Bolesław the Brave* by Wyspiański have come down to our times. They tell us of his preferences in stage design. The sketches are realistic and are based on historical data and historical research (Wyspiański was familiar with the concepts of the theatre of Duke von Meiningen). At the same time, they relate to folk art motifs, here seen in a stylized version. Painting and the graphic arts of the Modernist period must have exercised an influence on Wyspiański's tastes in art.

The quality of stage design improved noticeably at the Cracow theatre in the days when Ludwik Solski was director of the theatre. At this time, Karol Frycz, a man who was not only endowed with talent in the plastic arts but who was also an expert on the theatre, began to exercise an influence for the first time. Frycz started his career in the Cracow "Zielony balonik" (The Green Balloon) cabaret where he designed terribly funny puppets for the satirical programmes. He later tested his powers in the Cracow theatre. When, together with Arnold Szyfman, Frycz moved to Warsaw, the *Polski* Theatre was established. Frycz designed the sets for *Irydion,* a play which inaugurated the *Polski* Theatre with a gala performance in 1913 and remained the leading stage designer of that theatre for over 20 years. He returned to Cracow shortly before the outbreak of the Second World War and took over the post of theatre director, a function he still performed in the first postwar season.

Frycz was very good at creating illusions. With the minimum of cost, he wrought miraculous palaces and rich drawing rooms on the stage. He was always sensitive to colour but his carefully composed sets and costumes always had the sharply drawn line of good graphic work. Frycz was also an excellent stage architect. He built his sets of light materials which imitated heavy wood and metal to perfection. He had learned many of the tricks of trade in the Orient where he stayed a few years as cultural attaché of the Polish Embassy in Tokyo. The technique and achievement of the Japanese and Chinese theatres were not unknown to him. He tried to transplant what he had learned to the Polish stage. He had an infallible sense of style. His stage sets were pastiches of the art styles current in the period in which the action of the play took place. Significant in this respect were his sets to *Le Mariage de Figaro* by Beaumarchais inspired by the pictures of

Watteau and Fragonard, and his striking sets for Roman Brandstaetter's play about Rembrandt called
Return of the Prodigal Son. Frycz conjured on the stage
pictures of the great Dutch artist, composing furniture,
costumes, shades and light so as to give a perfect
illusion of the original. Frycz did not paint his sets but
improvised them on stage, selecting authentic furniture,
props and costumes with infallible genius. Being an
authority on Polish architecture and customs, he was
able to provide stage settings for *Pan Jowialski* and
other Fredro comedies in which the interiors and architecture of Polish manor houses, with which Frycz was
familiar since early youth, sprang to life on stage under
his hand.

Another leading stage designer of the *Polski* Theatre
was Wincenty Drabik. While Frycz constructed sets as
an architect would and possessed an expert knowledge
of the style and customs of the past that recalled the
works of the stage designer Berard in this respect, while
he designed costumes with the surehanded precision of
a fashion dictator, Drabik was above all a painter of
great dynamism and breadth of vision. He did not draw
with a fine line but painted large panoramas, with large
splashes of colour. His stage designs were more suitable
to plays based on fantasy or on fable rather than to
dramas where the style of the architecture and the
atmosphere of the period of the action had to be trans-
lated into the stage.

Two stage designers of the next generation, Andrzej
Pronaszko and Władysław Daszewski, emerged at the
top in the twenties and the thirties. In the twenties,
Pronaszko had connections with the Formists, a group
of Cracow painters who subscribed to the then
fashionable Cubism and Futurism. At first he designed

sets and costumes with his brother Zbigniew, a remarkable colorist who later gave up stage work and devoted himself completely to painting. The Pronaszko brothers worked with Schiller at the Bogusławski Theatre. Later, Andrzej Pronaszko collaborated with Schiller in the Lvov and Warsaw theatres. Andrzej Pronaszko had a sense of the geometrical. His designs took account of staging and action because he always thought in terms of the theatre. He carefully read the plays for which he was to design the settings, discussed the staging ideas with the director and in the end produced designs of immense plasticity which at the same time were ideal planes of action. Andrzej Pronaszko liked to build up the stage with the intention of having the action take place at several levels so as to add variety to stage movement. He was a stern and grave man, with a preference for brown and dark colour that did not admit the sun or the brilliant hues of the south. Among his most famous stage designs were the sets for *Fore-fathers' Eve* directed by Schiller. Pronaszko's backdrop for the entire play was a hill with three crosses on its crest. It represented the Three Crosses Hill in Vilna and was at the same time a metaphor of Polish martyrology, the underlying meaning of the masterpiece by Mickiewicz.

The bulk of Andrzej Pronaszko's work was done in the period of People's Poland. Among his best was the scenery for Lope de Vega's *Sheep well* directed by Bronisław Dąbrowski (the most striking feature was the forest which, though wholly deprived of naturalistic characteristics, nevertheless gave the impression of a wood in a southern country), for Szaniawski's *Two Theatres* directed by Edmund Wierciński (a remarkable idea of paper helmets for the young boys fighting for the freedom of Warsaw, emphasizing the tragic situation in which the small unarmed defenders of Warsaw faced the armour bristling regular troops of the Nazis). Upon moving to Warsaw, Pronaszko provided attractive settings for the Lithuanian writer Baltushis' *The Cocks Crow*. In Warsaw Pronaszko collaborated with Bohdan Korzeniewski and cooperated for the last time with Leon Schiller, taking an active creative part in the staging of Vsevolod Ivanov's *The Armoured Train*. Later, he provided the excellent designs for the sets to *The Madwomen of Chaillot* by Giraudoux, Wyspiański's *The Wedding* at the *Dramatyczny* Theatre of Warsaw and Słowacki's *Beatrix Cenci* directed by Jerzy Kreczmar. His design for the *Undivine Comedy* was never used while his sets for Musset's *Le Chandelier* were realized only after his death.

Władysław Daszewski is quite a different artistic personality from Andrzej Pronaszko. One was struck by the power of expression, of his always three dimensional sets. Daszewski, on other hand, preferred the two dimensional plane. The fact that he began as a graphic artist is clearly evident in his designs for the stage. Daszewski was a satirist and drew cartoons for the satirical weekly *Szpilki*. Unlike Pronaszko, he liked bright and serene colours: rich bronzes, blues, pinks and greens. Pronaszko was a Romanticist born too late for his time. He had grown up under the influence of the highly charged visions of Mickiewicz. Daszewski was a Neo-Realist, sharing a kinship with contemporary poetry and the style of new objectivity. Pronaszko was passionate and violent, Daszewski was cool and sceptical. Pronaszko was brutal, Daszewski — a man of moderation and fine esthetic tastes.

Daszewski's designs for *The Pickwick Club* (adaptation of the Pickwick Papers) at the *Polski* Theatre of Warsaw won wide acclaim before the last war. The Dickensian style suited Daszewski admirably. He had an affinity for the humour of the English writer, for his subtle lyricism and sceptical world outlook. Daszewski did his best work in the early postwar years, a time when he worked in close cooperation with Leon Schiller. It was then that he produced his pastel sets for *The Cracovians and the Mountaineers,* the brilliantly colourful settings for *The Tempest,* the dark and gloomy decorations for *Celestina* (an exception in Daszewski's work). Later, Daszewski provided the design for Gorky's *Yegor Bulichev and Others* which he maintained in his favourite bronze shades. In the fifties he did the sets for *Waiting for Godot* at the *Współczesny* Theatre of Warsaw, directed by Jerzy Kreczmar. But the guess is that perhaps his best design were the settings for Jan Potocki's *Parady* (Cavalcades) at the studio theatre of the *Dramatyczny* in Warsaw. Gay and frothy in effect, the sets exuded the atmosphere and elegance of the age of Enlightenment. The scenery provided insights into an age when this diversion of a rich aristocrat and talented writer was composed.

The fact that Karol Frycz, as Andrzej Pronaszko and Władysław Daszewski, was a director of the most important theatre of Poland testifies to the role stage designers have played for a long time in the life of the Polish theatre. Frycz headed the Słowacki Theatre of Cracow, Pronaszko reopened the *Stary* Theatre of Cracow after the war, and Daszewski was for a time director of the *Narodowy* Theatre of Warsaw.

Of later stage designers, whose work was as diversified as that of their predecessors, the most eminent role falls to Jan Kosiński. He belongs to the generation of artists who started their career just before the Second World War but whose activity in the theatre took place in the period of People's Poland. To some extent Kosiński continues along the same line as Frycz, although he is much more modern. Yet though he keeps abreast of all the latest trends and movements in art and in contemporary literature, his work remains nearly classical. Always flawless in composition, his sets are sleek in atmosphere and colour. Although he is not unfamiliar with the theatre of the absurd and with the dramatic avant-garde of the fifties and sixties, he remains concrete and lucid in the sets he designs for these plays.

Kosiński provided what may be the perfect setting for *The Good Woman of Setzuan* by Brecht largely contributing, by his ability to grasp the sense of the play, to its success. Using bamboo screens, Kosiński created the impression of a true Chinese background without depriving the play of its universal appeal. He also provided very fine sets for *Prometheus Bound* by Aeschylus, to Racine's *Phèdre,* to Shakespeare's *Hamlet,* Sartre's *The Flies,* Ionesco's *The Chairs* (Les Chaises) and above all to Dürrenmatt's *The Visit.* In the last production, Kosiński created to perfection the atmosphere of a small German town. In contrast, his sets for Sartre's *Le Diable et le Bon Dieu* and for Ghelderode's *La Ballade du Grand Macabre,* as well as for a number of classical and contemporary plays have breadth and scope. He demonstrated his knowledge of Polish style and of the Polish national tradition in his sets for *Kroniki królewskie* (Royal Chronicles), a montage of fragments selected from the verses and plays of Wyspiański made by Ludwik René which speaks of important events in the history of Poland.

Jan Kosiński plays an active role in the management of the *Dramatyczny* Theatre. He does not restrict himself to his work as stage designer but also exercises an influence on the repertory and its realization, hence upon the development of this important theatre.

If Kosiński may be recognized as heir to Frycz, then Tadeusz Kantor and Józef Szajna may be said to be the pupils and heirs of Andrzej Pronaszko. Kantor more than Szajna follows in the footsteps of his master. He is violent and gives little thought to aesthetic proportion, he is gloomy and expressive while his stage constructions are large in size, stressing his preference for geometric form. Kantor is, however, above all a painter conducting experiments in the theatre. His most notable works were the stage design for *Saint Joan* by Shaw at the *Stary* Theatre of Cracow (directed by Władysław Krzemiński) and the very original stage sets for Ionesco's *Rhinoceros*.

Józef Szajna has gone much farther than Kantor (who has abandoned stage design some years ago). At first he worked with Krystyna Skuszanka and Jerzy Krasowski at the *Ludowy* theatre in Nowa Huta. His first works were surrealistic, notably the fine sets for John Steinbeck's *Of Mice and Men*. The idea was a very simple one: Szajna suspended gnarled and twisted tree logs above an empty stage with a floor slanting sideways to create a mood of foreboding and evil as they dangle above the heads of the characters on stage. Using one simple element and blowing it up to unnatural size, Szajna provided an excellent setting for *Forefathers' Eve* seen at Nowa Huta. He placed a huge ladder on an empty stage. Konrad, disputing with God and the people, climbs the rungs to the top only to catapult from the soaring heights of exultation and elation to the hard earth below. Szajna sets out deliberately to shatter the illustion of the stage. He professes a programme of anti-aesthetics and an admiration of ugliness. He drapes the stage in rags to create an allusion to the disordered and revolting ugliness of the world. Józef Szajna succeeded Krystyna Skuszanka and Jerzy Krasowski as director of the *Ludowy* Theatre at Nowa Huta. He is now free to produce his weird visions with no restriction or control. The productions put on by the artist and stage director instance, the *Khorodnichy* (Town Bailiff) ran around were indeed out of the common run. In *Revizor* for in a torn uniform while a goat, taken straight out of a picture by Chagall, wandered incongruously about the stage. The root cause of Szajna's anti-aesthetic vision lies in his past which has conditioned the artist to view the world as he does. His is an obsession carried out of the concentration camp of Auschwitz where he was confined as a very young man. Tadeusz Hołuj's *Puste pole* (The Empty Field), a play set in Auschwitz many years after the war, served Szajna as excellent material for an imagination tainted by suffering. The play tells the story of former camp prisoners who arrive at the place of their former incarceration. Some of them are gold hunters come to look for treasures buried in the field of death. The grim subject enabled Szajna to make an awe-inspiring statement. For Wyspiański's *Acropolis* directed by Jerzy Grotowski, he also set the action in a concentration camp. Once again Szajna produced striking settings. The two productions bear out the fact that the artist can speak only of suffering and the martyrdom of modern man. He does so in every design he produces, no matter what theatre he is connected with. Witness his design for *Wariat i zakonnica* (The

Madman and the Nun) by S. I. Witkiewicz at the *Dramatyczny* Theatre and for the same author's *Nowe wyzwolenie* (The New Liberation) at the *Stary* Theatre of Cracow, the sets for Mayakovsky's *Bath* and Bryll's *Regarding November* at Katowice and even the stage designs for Sean O'Casey's comedy *Purple Dust* where the sets were at odds with the action. Szajna's design for the stage to the Sheffield production of *Macbeth* was a signal success. In this interpretation Macbeth was cast as a criminal, as a man responsible for genocide. Szajna's settings remind us of the suffering of contemporary man and extract a universal meaning out of Shakespeare's tragedy. This was also Szajna's approach to Goethe's *Faust* at the *Polski* Theatre of Warsaw. The noted stage designer is now turning his attention to stage directing because he feels that stage design and directing are one inseparable whole.

The folk trend occupies a separate and distinct position in the area of stage design in Poland. It harks back to early peasant and plebeian art. The leading representatives are Andrzej Stopka and Adam Kilian. Andrzej Stopka, whose main gifts are drawing and cartoons, was born at the Podhale foothill region. Understandably, he fell in love with the lovely art of the mountain folk of Poland. He gave an artistic translation of the art in the highly imaginative sets for *The Caucasian Chalk Circle* taking the Tatras and the Podhale rather the Georgia as a background for the action. For many years afterwards, Stopka did not seem to find the right formula for his interests in folk art. He did produce very fine sets for *Liberation,* directed by Bronisław Dąbrowski, but achieved his effect not by introducing folk elements of design but by a large abstract action painting which he used as a backdrop

Józef Szajna — sketch of stage design for Gounod's *Faust*

Jan Kosiński — sketch of stage design for de Ghelderode's *La Ballade du Grand Macabre*

Ewa Starowieyska — sketch of stage design for Gogol's *Marriage*

Andrzej Stopka — sketch of stage design for *The History of the Lord's Glorious Resurrection* by Mikołaj of Wilkowiecko

• Krzysztof Pankiewicz — stage design for *Il Combatimento di Tancredi e Clorinda* by Monteverdi

Adam Kilian — sketch of stage design for Wyspiański's *The Wedding*

*Costume design for Fre-
dro's* The Revenge

Theatre poster for Gałczyński's *Night of Miracles*

Theatre poster for Mayakovsky's *The Bath*

Theatre poster for Słowacki's *Fantazy*

Scene from a Wrocław pantomime production

to Konrad's dialogue with masks. Not until he began working with Kazimierz Dejmek did Stopka find the motivation to express himself fully on stage and to discover the best outlet for his talents. He did his best work in the early Polish plays *The History of the Lord's Glorious Resurrection* and *The Life of Joseph*. Stopka modelled himself on the old style folk puppet theatre to give two very different versions of it. The result was electrifying.

Adam Kilian takes a rather different attitude toward Polish folk art. While Stopka in his adaptations of folk motifs departs fom the originals, they serve him as an inspiration, Kilian stylized the folk motifs consciously without losing anything of the primitive simplicity. Kilian began his career as stage designer in the puppet theatre. He later brought the naive realism of the puppet theatre and folk art to the dramatic theatre. It made a refreshing change from the traditional conventions of stage design in this type of play. Among Kilian's most outstanding designs for the dramatic theatre was the setting for Bogusławski's *The Cracovians and the Mountaineers* directed by Bronisław Dąbrowski. It seemed that after Daszewski's remarkable sets, it would be difficult to find a better setting for the play. Kilian proved himself a match to the challenge. He created a setting composed of paper cut outs and toys sold at country fairs, hence the wagons and horses, the caps and crops one can buy in the villages of Cracow and Podhale. Kilian produced some exciting sets for the plays of Ernest Bryll, hence for the show composed of Christmas carols called *Over Hills, Over Clouds* at the *Ludowy* Theatre of Nowa Huta and to his song play about Janosik *Painted on Glass* at the Słowacki Theatre of Cracow and other Polish theatres. Kilian has become the accepted specialist of Bryll's folk plays. *Painted on Glass* must have suited him admirably, for it was Kilian who first introduced on the stage the pictures painted on glass of the Polish mountaineers and it was Kilian who had the original idea of using reeds and mats woven of reeds on the stage as a new and valuable material. Not only does it have a very interesting texture but due to its plasticity can be easily modelled.

The painterly trend in Polish stage sets deserves high praise. The three leading representatives are: Andrzej Majewski, Krzysztof Pankiewicz and Marian Kołodziej. Majewski and Pankiewicz, with their rich pictorial imagination and love of lush colour, recall in their work the style of Wincenty Drabik. Both Majewski and Pankiewicz go in for modern techniques in painting and both are abstract artists. The results on stage are very interesting. The sets designed by Majewski and Pankiewicz are notable for atmosphere. The costumes create bright splashes of colour in a setting with which they orchestrate in a harmonious composition. The stage designs of Majewski and Pankiewicz suit the convention of the opera, ballet and the lyric theatre and the two artists have had their greatest success in this area.

Marian Kołodziej gives broad sweeping areas of intense colour of no specific shape that are strongly reminiscent of expressionism. Kołodziej was also a prisoner of Auschwitz. Although one cannot discover any sign of this past in the subject of his stage design, yet it comes through clearly in the sad and pensive colour schemes he uses. Among his finest works are: the sets to *The Rich Man and the Beggar* by the Anonym of Gdańsk, directed at the *Wybrzeże* Theatre by Tadeusz Minc and sets to *Undivine Comedy, The Seagull, Norwid* and *Beniowski* at the *Narodowy*

Mieczysława Ćwiklińska as Fiokla in Gogol's *Marriage* — caricature by Edward Głowacki

Theatre of Warsaw. Kołodziej and Adam Hanuszkiewicz have found a common language. The director likes rich colours and Kołodziej's concentrated and poetic stage painting.

A new development in Polish stage design is the large number of women who practice this art. At first, Teresa Roszkowska and Jadwiga Przeradzka were the only women of note in the field. Today, there is a whole galaxy of talented women designers. Foremost among these is Zofia Wierchowicz, stage designer and director. She has produced an all-purpose setting, a structure based on the principles of the original Shakespearean theatre, which with a few changes can be adapted to all the dramas of Shakespeare. Then there is Ewa Starowieyska, a very talented woman stage designer, who has worked with Erwin Axer for many years. Krystyna Zachwatowicz has had successes at home and abroad with her surrealistic scenery (the remarkable setting for *The Marriage* by Gombrowicz, *Leyzorek Roytshvanets* according to Ehrenburg as well as *As You Like It* by Shakespeare directed by Skuszanka and many others). Zofia Pietrusińska has done very good sets for *The Water Hen* and *Jan Karol Maciej Wścieklica* at the *Narodowy* Theatre. Urszula Gogulska did a very competent job on the sets for Dostoyevsky's *Uncle's Dream* directed by Lidia Zamkow. Mention must also be made of Lidia Minticz (she works with Jerzy Skarżyński), Liliana Jankowska (who has been working for some time with Antoni Tota) and Teresa Ponińska. The head stage designer of the Polish television is Xymena Zaniewska. Among the youngest generation Barbara Stopka and Joanna Braun — both of Cracow — represent the women stage designers.

Among the Polish designers of the older generation

one must mention Otto Axer, of the middle generation Andrzej Cybulski and Stanisław Bąkowski and the very gifted and original scenographer Kazimierz Wiśniak. Among the new generation of designers is Łukasz Burnat (who works with Maciej Prus), Piotr Piaskowski and a group of the youngest designers. Daniel Mróz, noted illustrator, betrays his major interest for the theatre occasionally. Notable among his designs were the sets for Witold Wandurski's *Śmierć na gruszy* (Death in the Pear Tree), directed by Józef Szajna. Wojciech Krakowski uses the collage technique in his designs. He was most successful perhaps with his sets for *An Old Woman Sitting* by Różewicz, directed by Jarocki.

It is abundantly clear that stage design represents a strong side of the Polish theatre.

For a time there was some fear lest stage design break away from the theatre and become an independent branch of art which will not wish to assist the director or the actors. The fears seem to have been dispelled for the moment. Stage designers do not have the ambition to outshine the text or to discount it. More and more leading artists are becoming interested in the theatre and cooperating with it, to take the most recent example of the famous sculptor Władysław Hasior who has been cooperating steadily with the Wrocław theatre since 1970. He designed very striking settings for Molière's *Don Juan* directed by Jerzy Krasowski. Then there is Krzysztof Pankiewicz who in 1970 directed and designed the sets for *Don Juan* at Zielona Góra.

CHAPTER VI

ACTORS

The Polish theatre entered the postwar period surrounded by the glory of great acting. On the whole, the acting was realistic, marked by good craftsmanship and based on a perceptive analysis of character and keen observation of life. The appearance of the actors, their faces and the way they moved were adapted and transformed to mould a character. Though aware of more recent trends in the stage arts, the actors relied most heavily on the Stanislavsky method. Several styles of stage acting may be distinguished in the Polish theatre.

Osterwa represented the introspective psychological school of thought combined with the ardour and charm of the romantic hero, although he was not deprived of talent as a character actor.

Jaracz was a past master of the introverted, reflective, though highly expressive style. He was good in tragedy and in comedy alike. His comic characters always had the touch of tragedy about them. He was the best Polish Captain of Köpenick, Schweik and Arnold in Molière's *L'Ecole des Femmes*. He liked to play the common, simple little people, to uncover the great tragedies of which no one would have suspected them.

Zelwerowicz, with his natural endowments, was best suited for character parts. He was a big burly man in complete control of his massive body, with a magnificent large ringing voice, incomparable as a comic. However, he usually endowed his characters with weird and often pathological traits. The most perfect example of his skills was Porphiri in *Crime and Punishment.*

Junosza-Stępowski was perhaps the best in the technical sense. His potrayals were sharply drawn, he was a discerning observer and excellent imitator, modelling his face and body with masterful virtuosity. His every movement and gesture was clear-cut and evocative. He was admirable in the great tragedies as well as in drawing room dramas and comedies. He created an unforgettable portrait of the Chamberlain in Rittner's *Crazy Jacob.* As Henry IV in the play of Pirandello he gave a marvellous portrayal of a man poised terrifyingly on the brink of madness, feeling nothing but hate for the cringing baseness of the world.

Finally there was Józef Węgrzyn, a remarkable romantic actor, the personification of charm and lightness, and Jerzy Leszczyński who was at his best in the plays of Fredro and in French comedy.

The war decimated the ranks od Poland's great stars of the stage. Jaracz died in 1945, Junosza-Stępowski died before the end of the war as did Stanisława Wysocka. Osterwa died in 1947. Węgrzyn survived the war but he was only a shadow of his former self, sinking to smaller and smaller supporting roles. Karol Awentowicz had lost none of his powers. He headed a few theatres in People's Poland and was very busy acting. But his acting style was dated and not until shortly before he died did Adwentowicz's talent shine again in a straightforward and forceful performance of Horsztyński.

The first fifteen years of the theatre in People's Poland were dominated by the talent and craftsmanship of two great character actors — Jan Kurnakowicz and

Jacek Woszczerowicz. It was these two fine artists who enjoyed the greatest popularity, not counting Ludwik Solski of course who was a kind of biological phenomenon. He toured Poland and appeared on the stage in his nineties and celebrated 80 years on the stage and his 100th birthday appearing as Dyndalski in *The Revenge* at the *Polski* Theatre of Warsaw.

Kurnakowicz was a fiery and energetic character actor of extraordinary talent. His acting style was closely related to the Russian school. As one would expect, he was excellent in the Russian repertory. His greatest single portrayal was that of *Khorodniczy* in Gogol's *Revizor*. The strength and creative imagination, the lacerating irony and knowledge of human psychology that went into the character, caused the Russian theatre authorities to express their admiration for him. Kurnakowicz was also magnificient as Phamusov in Griboyedov's *The Misfortune of Being Clever*, as Schvandia in Trenev's *Lubov Yarovaya* and as Podkolesin in Gogol's *Marriage*. Aware of the artistic preferences of Kurnakowicz and of his drawling eastern accent, the critics were sceptical when he was cast as the Cup-Bearer, an epitome a Polish squire, in Fredro's *The Revenge*. The director Bohdan Korzeniewski was proved right in betting on his talent. Kurnakowicz was good and in some ways, even superb as the Cup-Bearer, though unlike any of the characterizations given before him. Among his finest roles were Bottom in a *Midsummer Night's Dream* and as Doolittle in *Pygmalion*. His last great role, one which will forever remain in our memory, was that of the Grand Duke Constantin in Słowacki's *Kordian* at the *Narodowy* Theatre directed by Erwin Axer. The leading role was played by Tadeusz Łomnicki, yet it was Kurnakowicz who outshone

Jan Kurnakowicz as Podkolesin in Gogol's *Marriage* — caricature by Edward Głowacki

everybody. The most memorable scene was the one in which the Grand Duke watches Kordian leap across a high barricade. The Duke had made a wager with the tsar that one of his soldiers will make the jump. We see him observing the leap with all his muscles tensed like a gambler whose very honour is at stake. He expressed everything in that scene: Constantin's passion, he loved horses and was proud of his Polish cavalry, his hate of the tsar to whom he had to surrender the throne though he never accepted his superiority, his gambling passion and his joy of triumph. Kurnakowicz hit upon a marvellous device. Leaning forward slightly, as if following the flight of the horse and rider over the barricade, he slapped his thighs rhythmically with his hand. The closer the victory the quicker and louder the slaps, capped after the leap with a hoarse animal-like laughter of a gratified despot and tyrant.

Woszczerowicz was an actor of a different order. Less than average in height, he had to overcome many hardships and obstacles before he gained a position in the theatre. Woszczerowicz began his career in the *Reduta,* but Osterwa did not see a future for him on the stage and advised him to look for another profession. Woszczerowicz remained adamant in his resolve and already before the war was recognized as one of the leading actors of the Polish stage. He gave his best performance as Socrates in Ludwik Hieronim Morstin's *Obrona Ksantypy* (The Defense of Xantippe). After the war he played Łatka in Fredro's *Dożywocie* (Life Annuity). For a few years after that he worked closely with Bohdan Korzeniewski, giving his best performance as Tarelkin in a play by Sukhovo-Kobylin and as Sganarel in Molière's *Don Juan* and Papkin in *The Revenge.* He attained the heights of his acting powers in the late fifties. The two portrayals he gave then decided about his eminent position as actor. These were Richard III in Shakespeare's historical chronicle and as Joseph K. in Kafka's *The Trial*. Two totally different interpretations of two unusual characters. As Richard III Woszczerowicz was a personification of perversion and evil, of criminal predilections and hate, and contempt for the world. There was something of the jester about him, of a cruel jester that made one think of Nero. There was also something tragic about his Richard. He showed him as a man completely alienated, incapable of any contacts with the people around him, people he hated and was afraid of. Woszczerowicz made the best of his small stature in this role. The spectator was made to believe that it accounted for Richard's inferiority complex with regard to his tall cousins and English lords and for his frustrated ambitions with regard to women. He sought to compensate his sense of inferiority in acts of violence, in crime and in a kind of self-attrition.

His Joseph K. was a different man. Here, Woszczerowicz played a terrified, hounded little man, a victim of a mysterious force and power which tortures and destroys him without any given reason. The play was produced shortly after the political changes which occurred in Poland in 1956 and made a clear allusion to the fear and the danger to human personality in the era of the personality cult. Woszczerowicz was a helpless victim striving to preserve his dignity even when he has hit bottom.

Woszczerowicz later gave a very fine performance as King Ferrante in Montherlant's *Queen After Death* and in the title role of Pinter's *The Caretaker*. He invested the characters with weird eccentricities, a mark of his acting style. This feature of his style was brought out most forcibly perhaps in his television portrayal of a conductor of a phantom train wandering through the empty cars after a crack-up. His most memorable television role was that of an insignificant accountant who discovers the crimes of a famous author in Dürrenmatt's play *Autumn Evening* and as Captain of Köpenick in the television version of Zuckmayer's play. Woszczerowicz was considered the successor and continuator of Stefan Jaracz in the Polish theatre. During the last dozen or so years of his life he appeared at the *Ateneum* founded by Jaracz in what were to be the finest characterizations of his career.

Irena Eichlerówna, graduate of the Theatre School of Warsaw, made her debut in Vilna where she enjoyed her first success. She appeared in Lvov as Polly in Brecht's *The Threepenny Opera.*

Eichlerówna spent the war abroad finding asylum in Brazil. After the war she returned to Poland and at first appeared in Łódź where she played the title role in Maxwell Anderson's *Joan of Lorraine* and later drew acclaim as Phèdre in Racine's tragedy and as Mrs Warren in Shaw's *Mrs Warren's Profession.* One of Eichlerówna's finest roles was Mother Courage in Bertolt Brecht's play.

Eichlerówna has a magnificent resonant voice, ranging from a modulated but penetrating whisper to a ringing shout. With her commanding stage presence she holds the attention of the audience throughout the performance.

The lovely and graceful Elżbieta Barszczewska, a favourite with the Warsaw public, was at one time cast in the Polish Romantic repertory as the young and innocent girl from the country manor. Her most memorable roles were as Diana in *Fantazy* and as Lilla Weneda in a play of the same title.

Nina Andrycz is an excellent technician but she has an essentially cool and aloof, though very expressive and evocative style. She will always remain in our memory as the aristocratic Miss Izabella Łęcka in the stage adaptation of *Lalka* (The Doll) by Prus.

The leading cerebral actor of the Polish theatre is Jan Kreczmar, a highly talented character actor with a penchant for comedy (though he rarely took recourse to it). He was a remarkable Count Wacław in Fredro's *Man and Wife*, Chatski in *The Misfortune of Being Clever*, the theatre director in *Two Theatres* and the tormented husband in *Who's Afraid of Virginia Woolf?*

Marian Wyrzykowski, who appeared in the great Romantic and poetic plays such as *Hamlet* and *Kordian*, and who had given interesting comic impersonation, may be included among the leading actors of his day.

A group of very talented young actors who were to win fame in People's Poland appeared on the stage side by side with actors who had established their position in the theatre before the war. The young actors got their beginning in the theatres of Cracow and Łódź in the first postwar years. In the fifties most of them joined the theatres of Warsaw. Gustaw Holoubek, Tadeusz Łomnicki, Zofia Rysiówna, Halina Mikołajska and Aleksandra Śląska made their debuts in Cracow. Jan Świderski (who made his debut just before the war in Poznań), Zofia Mrozowska and Andrzej Łapicki appeared in the Łódź theatres. They rose to eminence in the Polish theatre in the course of a decade and, as the great actors of the prewar period passed away, the new generation took their place.

Although it cannot be said that they succeeded to the

roles of their famous predecessors, yet here again we have a wide diversity of acting styles represented by the individual stage personalities, a large range of talents and tastes.

Gustaw Holoubek brings out the thought behind the text. He doesn't externalize (act) the words but speaks his lines with an awareness that he is standing beside the character, commenting his words and actions. He has remarkable expressive eyes, a resonant though not an especially big voice and a subtle winning smile. He is best remembered as Judge Custo in Ugo Betti's *Corruption at the Palace of Justice*, as Goetz in Sartre's *Le Diable et le Bon Dieu*, as Father Riccardo in Hochhuth's *The Deputy*, directed by Dejmek, hence a series of roles of the contemporary repertory. He captivated the audiences with the magic of his delivery as Konrad in *Forefathers' Eve*. His rendition of the Great Improvisation, the key monologue of this masterpiece of Polish national literature, surpassed anything done by the actors who have ever appeared in the part. Holoubek also turned in a fine performance as Richard II in the play by Shakespeare. He was less successful as Hamlet and King Oedipus. The classical repertory suits him best when he relates its problems to the issues of our day.

Jan Świderski is primarily a marvellous technican. No other Polish actor can alter and transform his appearance to the extent he does. He represents the line of actors stemming from Junosza-Stępowski whose genuine successor he is today. He follows Junosza-Stępowski in the role of Chamberlain in Rittner's *Crazy Jacob*, though his craftsmanship lacks some of the excellence of his famous model. His acting style is brusque and expressive. He is a character actor who pays great attention to all the psychological subtleties, to the harmony between inner meaning and external form. He first attracted attention as Baron in Gorky's *The Lower Depths* directed by Leon Schiller. His next spectacular realization came as Romulus the Great in a play of the same name by Dürrenmatt. Świderski reached the peak of his form as an actor in the sixties, appearing at the *Ateneum* theatre in a couple of remarkable characterizations. Most noteworthy were: the part of old Salomon in Arthur Miller's *The Price* and as the Chamberlain in *Crazy Jacob*. Świderski is also a noted television actor. His Voievoda in Słowacki's *Mazepa* had inordinate force and inner strength. Świderski's later *tour de force* is the role of Cup Bearer in Fredro's *The Revenge*. In a most unconventional reading of the part, he plays it with roaring passion, without sentimentality but with enormous expressive power.

Tadeusz Łomnicki won recognition when still a very young actor in Katowice and Cracow appearing as Franio in Perzyński's *Szczęście Frania* (Franio's Luck) and as the Boy from the Rain in Szaniawski's *Two Theatres*. He played Mazepa as well at this time. He was acclaimed the new Jaracz. Łomnicki, with his rather thickset and short body, does not have the physical endowments of our ideal of the Romantic hero. Yet he played Kordian at the *Narodowy* Theatre and passed the test with flying colours. Yet he realized that he would not find the most suitable roles for himself in the Romantic repertory. Łomnicki is a character actor, with a penchant for tragedy or even tragi-comedy. He has a magnificent voice, with a greater range and power than any other actor in the Polish theatre. He is also a splendid craftsman whose talent shines in the contemporary repertory. That explains his resounding success as Arturo Ui in Brecht's *The Resistible Rise of Arturo Ui* which is perhaps the best part in his entire career. Łomnicki gave here a display of his talents in a pyrotechnics of delivery that ranged from an evil whisper to a roar. His voice recalled the guttural rantings of the star ham of them all Hitler who held the crowds spellbound with hysterical rhetoric. Łomnicki was an excellent Glumov in Ostrovsky's *A Rogue's Memoirs* directed by Tovstonogov. He gave a subtle up-dated portrait of a hypocrite and a careerist. He turned in a very good performance as the lead in Osborne's *Inadmissible Evidence* directed at the *Współczesny* Theatre of Warsaw by Lindsay Anderson.

Łomnicki's interests are not restricted to acting alone. He has tried his hand at writing plays, his play *Noah and His Menagerie* was played with great success, he studied stage directing and has directed occasionally at the *Współczesny*. He is above all one of the foremost actors of the Polish film. He has appeared in *Pokolenie* (The Generation) and *Niewinni czarodzieje* (The Innocent Sorceres) both directed by Andrzej Wajda. Most recently he has won enormous popularity and admiration as Pan Wołodyjowski in the film and the television serial based on the novel of Henryk Sienkiewicz. The film was a box office success and Łomnicki became the youth idol of the country and the actor of the year.

Right after the war a trio of actresses, Zofia Rysiówna, Halina Mikołajska and Aleksandra Śląska, appeared in Cracow. Zofia Rysiówna, a vivacious brunette of great dramatic power, won great acclaim as Balladyna in Słowacki's play and then appeared as Diana in *Fantazy* directed by Juliusz Osterwa. In Cracow she played next

The plays of Stanisław Ignacy Witkiewicz are popular with the Polish theatres. Wanda Łuczycka and Jan Kobuszewski in *Jan Karol Maciej Wścieklica* at the *Narodowy* Theatre of Warsaw.

Zofia Małynicz and Tadeusz Fijewski in Stanisław Grocho-wiak's Boys at the *Kameralny* Theatre of Warsaw

Aleksandra Śląska and **Krzysztof Chamiec** in Chekhov's *Uncle Vanya*, directed by Kazimierz Dejmek at the *Ateneum*

Elżbieta Barszczewska as Nora at the *Kameralny* Theatre

Irena Eichlerówna and Kazimierz Opaliński in Chekhov's *The Seagull*

Twilight, a play by Isaac Babel, directed by Jerzy Jarocki and with stage sets by Urszula Gogulska. Maria Bednarska and Wiktor Sadecki. Produced at the *Stary* Theatre of Cracow

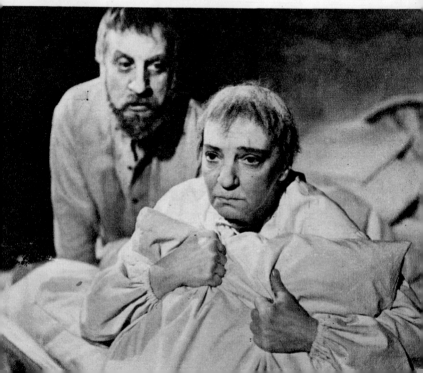

The Cobblers by Stanisław Ignacy Witkiewicz directed by Maciej Prus and with stage sets by Łukasz Burnat, at the Bogusławski Theatre of Kalisz

Wiesław Gołas (Papkin) and Małgorzata Niemirska (Clara) in
The Revenge

Jan Świderski (Cupbearer) and Gustaw Holoubek (Notary) in
Fredro's *The Revenge* at the *Dramatyczny* Theatre of Warsaw.

Scene from Ernest Bryll's *Regarding November* directed by Bronisław Dąbrowski and with stage sets by Jan Kosiński. The Słowacki Theatre of Cracow

An Old Woman Sitting by Tadeusz Różewicz directed by Jerzy Jarocki and with stage sets by Wojciech Krakowski at the Współczesny Theatre of Wrocław

Laurencia in Lope de Vega's *Sheep well* and as Masha in Chekhov's *The Three Sisters*. In 1949 Rysiówna joined the Poznań theatre and later came to Warsaw where she played Katya Maslova in a stage adaptation of Tolstoy's *Resurrection* and Berenice in Racine's tragedy.

Halina Mikołajska made her first appearance on the professional stage while still a student at the theatre school. Edmund Wierciński selected her for the part of Euridice in Anna Świrszczyńska's *Orpheus*. The young student actress acquitted herself so well that she drew wide attention. With her physical fragility and subtle charm she soon became the most outstanding lyrical actress and tragedienne on the Polish stage, giving a memorable performance as Irina in Chekchov's *The Three Sisters*, followed by Ruth in Kruczkowski's *The Germans* (the Wrocław production). She moved to Warsaw in 1950 and joined the Polish Theatre company where she gave a remarkable characterization of a young seduced girl in the newly discovered play by Żeromski called *Grzech* (The Sin). Her finest role in this period was Ethel Rosenberg in Leon Kruczkowski's *Julius and Ethel*. In 1955 Mikołajska joined the *Dramatyczny* Theatre of Warsaw where she appeared as Rachel in Wyspiański's *The Wedding* followed by an unforgettable performance as Se Shui Ta in *The Good Woman of Setzuan* by Brecht. She was also very good as the old woman in Ionesco's *The Chairs*. In the sixties Mikołajska moved to the *Współczesny* Theatre and there gave two splendid performances, as Queen Elizabeth in Schiller's *Mary Stuart* and as the Mother in the play of the same title by Stanisław Ignacy Witkiewicz. With the years Mikołajska began to play different roles. The lyrical style now began to assume the sharpness of outline noted in character actors. She is a marvellous craftsman, with absolute control of her body. In the course of one play she can transform into an old woman and then back again into a lovely charming young woman (as in *Mother*).

Zofia Mrozowska has unusual charm and nobility, a classical beauty, lovely features and a soft lyrical expression. She made her debut in Łódź in the great Polish romantic repertory and in poetic plays. She later joined Axer's company and moved to Warsaw with his theatre where she remains as the leading actress to this day. Among her finest roles was the lead in Tennessee Williams' *The Glass Menagerie* (in Łódź) and later as Tatiana in Gorky's *The Townsfolk*, Viola in *Twelfth Night* and as Iphigenia in the play by Goethe. She was a tremendous success as Iphigenia proving that she is not only a sensitive and subtle actress but that she is also capable of power when speaking in the defence of freedom and peace. She was also a lovely Mary Stuart, her regal pride and honour untouched by the suffering and humiliation to which Elizabeth had sentenced her.

Aleksandra Śląska is a totally different type of actress. She is far less emotional but is an excellent craftsman, her acting controlled by her intellectual grasp of character. She is an artist of the modern school of acting withdrawn and in complete control of her body with an expressive face, sharply defined gestures and body movement. She is the feminine counterpart of Jan Świderski. After the first stage roles in Cracow, where this slight fair haired girl with Nordic features attracted interest, Śląska appeared in her first film role in *The Last Stage*. She played the part of a Nazi superintendent in the Auschwitz Concentration Camp. Her performance placed her among the top acting talents of Poland. She then moved to Warsaw and remained for many years at the *Współczesny* Theatre. Her biggest part in that period was Inga in Leon Kruczkowski's *Pierwszy dzień wolności* (The First Day of Freedom). In the sixties Śląska joined the *Ateneum* Theatre. Here she distinguished herself primarily as a character actress in contemporary French and American plays. She turned in a fine performance in Marcel Aymé's *La Tête des autres* and the title role in Montherlant's *Queen After Death*. She was able to display her talents to advantage in Faulkner's *Requiem for a Nun* and played the lead in Edward Albee's *Everything in the Garden*. She has also given a number of very good performances in the television theatre productions.

Acting talent flourishes in the theatre of People's Poland principally when it is placed under the guidance of eminent directors in the best theatre companies. The *Współczesny* Theatre Company is undoubtedly among their number. Next to Zofia Mrozowska, we have observed the maturation of such talents as Marta Lipińska, with her alluring and lyrical charm, as the character actor Tadeusz Fijewski, Henryk Borowski, Mieczysław Czechowicz, Czesław Wołłejko and Andrzej Łapicki, the matinée idol of the Polish theatre. Zbigniew Zapasiewicz revealed his talents here to move on later to the *Dramatyczny* Theatre and the character actress Barbara Krafftówna finds an opportunity to display her talents here.

In the sixties a very interesting company was formed at the *Powszechny* Theatre by Adam Hanuszkiewicz. The company later moved on to form the backbone of the *Narodowy* Theatre when Hanuszkiewicz became director there. Adam Hanuszkiewicz plays the first fiddle both as stage director and as actor. In the fifties, when he was still in Poznań, he was starred as Hamlet under Wilam Horzyca's direction. He also had a number of very successful roles in the television theatre. In his own company he gave an outstanding interpretation of the part of Raskolnikov in *Crime and Punishment*, of Konrad in *Liberation* and Robespierre in Büchner's *Danton's Death*, the title role in Molière's *Don Juan* and of Count Henryk in *The Undivine Comedy*. This tall man with the thin narrow face seems predestined for the leading roles in the Romantic and Neo-Romantic repertory. He reads verse admirably, the emotions clearly legible on his craggy face. If it can be said that Holoubek acts the thoughts then Hanuszkiewicz acts the emotions.

Mariusz Dmochowski is the foremost actor in his company. He is the exact psychic and physical antithesis of Hanuszkiewicz. Dmochowski is a tall, heavy broad-shouldered man. While Hanuszkiewicz is subtle in his acting style, Dmochowski represents brute force that may be at times vulgar and violent. Among Dmochowski's best parts at the *Powszechny* Theatre was Coriolanus and Wokulski in *The Doll* by Prus. At the *Narodowy* Theatre he gave a fine performance as Pankracy in *The Undivine Comedy* by Krasiński and as Polonius in *Hamlet*.

Zofia Kucówna's talents have also grown and matured at the *Narodowy* Theatre. While still at the *Powszechny* Theatre, she played Sonyechka Marmeladova in *Crime and Punishment* with spellbinding delicacy. At the *Narodowy* she was seen as Saint Joan in Shaw's play of the same title and as Queen Gertrude in *Hamlet*. Kucówna has a peasant-like simplicity, an innocence and fresh charm both in her acting and in her appearance.

Emilia Krakowska's talent first became apparent at the *Powszechny*. It was emerged in full at the *Narodowy* Theatre. Talented Szczecin actors, Włodzimierz Bednarski, Andrzej Kopiczyński and Maria Chwalibóg have joined the company. They had worked a few years in Szczecin under the guidance of Jan Maciejowski, gifted director of Shakespearean plays, with whom they moved to Warsaw. The *Narodowy* Theatre company also gained a fine actor in the person of Jerzy Kamas who came to Warsaw from Cracow where he had appeared successfully at the Słowacki Theatre.

But the greatest young talent to appear at the *Narodowy* Theatre is Daniel Olbrychski. He started out as a film actor, winning a star position by appearing mainly in Andrzej Wajda's films. Adam Hanuszkiewicz persuaded him to try the theatre. After a small but well done part in Fredro's comedy *Śluby panieńskie* (Maidens' Vows), Hanuszkiewicz decided to take the big risk and to cast Olbrychski as Hamlet. This was a big challenge and it seemed that the 25-year old actor, with no experience in the theatre, would fail to meet the demands of the role. His performance proved an unqualified success. He played Hamlet with the spontaneity of a modern young man. Finding in 1970 the key to the character, he spoke to modern youth as if Hamlet had been written for them and about them. He quickly transcended the lack of stage experience and technical skills of the craft, and captivated the audience with the genuine sincerity of his performance and the sheer power of his talent. He reinforced his position remarkably in the part of Bieniowski.

A number of actors achieved new heights of greatness

in the days when Kazimierz Dejmek was director of the *Narodowy*. Notable among them was Gustaw Holoubek and his masterful portrayal of Gustaw-Konrad in *Farefathers' Eve* as well as Wojciech Siemion who, though he had already attracted interest earlier in his career, was finally given the chance to display his original talent here. Siemion is perhaps the most outstanding peasant-folk type in the Polish theatre. Short of stature, with the features of a Polish peasant, Siemion speaks the peasant dialect like no other actor in the modern Polish theatre. A son of a peasant he had heard and spoken the dialect in his youth. A talented character actor, he has an understanding for peasant humour and poetry. He was excellent in a programme called *Wieża malowana* (The Painted Tower), based on a scenario provided by Ernest Bryll who also has a preference for folk poetry and likes to introduce it into his works. But he reached the heights of artistry at the *Narodowy* Theatre in Dejmek's production of the *History of the Lord's Glorious Resurrection* where he appeared in the role of Sorrowful Christ looking an exact image of the carved figure seen in the country roadside chapels. This was followed by the part of Joseph in *The Life of Joseph* and a small but very important role of Christ in Bruno Jasieński's *Słowo o Jakubie Szeli* (A Word about Jakub Szela). The talent of Ignacy Machowski emerged at the *Narodowy* Theatre in the days when Dejmek was its director. Machowski was with Dejmek already in Łódź. Other actors who rose to prominence were Jan Kobuszewski, Barbara Krafftówna, Barbara Rachwalska, Bogdan Baer and others.

The *Dramatyczny* (Dramatic) Theatre of the Capital City of Warsaw has a very competent company of actors.

At one time Jan Świderski and Halina Mikołajska were the unchallenged stars here. Today, the big wheel at the Dramatic Theatre is Gustaw Holoubek and a whole list of rising talents among artists of the middle generation. Notable among these is: Ignacy Gogolewski, a character actor with a talent ranging from tragedy and tragicomedy to comedy, Zbigniew Zapasiewicz, successor to Jan Kreczmar, the finest cerebral actor of the young generation and remarkable as Chatski in Griboyedov's *The Misfortune of Being Clever*. Then there is Wiesław Gołas — a great comic talent — and Małgorzata Niemirska, a recent graduate of the Warsaw school of the theatre who despite her young age has played ingenues with striking conviction and simplicity, as well as being a very alluring and attractive person on stage.

The leading actors at the *Ateneum* are Jan Świderski and Aleksandra Śląska. The company includes a group of gifted artists of the middle generation, notably Roman Wilhelmi, Jan and Marian Kociniak (excellent in character parts and in modern domestic plays). The actors who joined the *Ateneum* after leaving the *Narodowy* Theatre are: Barbara Rachwalska, Bogdan Baer and Stanisław Zaczyk, the latter one of the best actors of the middle generation whose talent attracted attention years ago in Cracow when he appeared as Konrad in *Liberation*. He is still waiting for his big part in Warsaw. One of the most reliable artists of the *Ateneum* company is Krzysztof Chamiec, for many years star of the Łódź theatres.

The *Polski* Theatre, once the first theatre of the land, has a dependable company of artists, with such celebrated actresses as Elżbieta Barszczewska and Nina Andrycz, who had been members of the theatre in its finest days, and a number of character actors such as

Bronisław Pawlik and Jan Kobuszewski, and finally Tadeusz Fijewski who moved here from the *Współczesny*.

The favourite Polish comedienne is Irena Kwiatkowska, star of the *Syrena* Theatre of Warsaw and television.

Not all the best stage actors are in the Warsaw theatres. We find them in other parts of Poland. Second in importance after Warsaw as a theatre centre is Cracow. The Słowacki Theatre has such fine stars of the stage as Zofia Jaroszewska and Maria Malicka, Leszek Herdegen and Marian Cebulski; the *Stary* Theatre can boast of a group of young actors whose talents developed under the guidance of Konrad Swinarski and Jerzy Jarocki, notable among these are Anna Seniuk (who moved to the *Ateneum* in 1970), Franciszek Pieczka (now at the *Dramatyczny* Theatre of Warsaw), Anna Polony, Marek Walczewski, Izabella Olszewska, Wiktor Sadecki and others. At the *Ludowy* Theatre of Nowa Huta, Krystyna Skuszanka and Jerzy Krasowski guided a group of actors to fame. Among the finest of these were Witold Pyrkosz, Ryszard Kotys and Ferdynand Matysiak. The leading actors of Wrocław are Igor Przegrodzki, Artur Młodnicki, Stanisław Michalik, Anna Lutosławska and finally Edward Lubaszenko whose talent has developed so nicely at the *Współczesny* Theatre. The Łódź theatres have a competent group of actors, notable among whom are Feliks Żukowski and Jerzy Przybylski. At the *Wybrzeże* Theatre Marek Okopiński, its director, has attracted a group of remarkable artists like Halina Winiarska, Stanisław Igar, Tadeusz Gwiazdowski and Bogusława Czosnowska. In Poznań there is the very interesting Tadeusz Wojtycha and gaining prominence in

Kazimierz Opaliński as Zevakin in Gogol's *Marriage* — caricature by Edward Głowacki

Szczecin is Michał Ulewicz who played Konrad in *Liberation,* the Journalist in *the Wedding* and Hamlet.

The Polish schools of the theatre in Warsaw, Cracow and Łódź are preparing young talents for the stage profession. The rest is achieved by practice and the expert guidance of stage directors. Young theatre artists are offered wide opportunities in their profession, especially in the smaller theatres where the standards are frequently very demanding. But even in Warsaw the young and frequently the beginners have a chance to appear in leading roles. This was true in the case of Anna Seniuk and Daniel Olbrychski as well as in the case of Andrzej Seweryn, Małgorzata Niemirska and Olgierd Łukaszewicz in recent years and before him of Marta Lipińska and Barbara Sołtysik, stars of the *Współczesny* Theatre.

It might be said that Polish actors are very good on the whole although they seem to remain in the shadow of stage directors and stage designers. Complaints are sometimes heard that training in acting technique is poor in quality, that teaching methods are obsolete and that no attempt is made to experiment in this area. In view of this situation, Jerzy Grotowski's Laboratory Theatre grows to first importance as a seedbed of new ideas. Grotowski's method is now being taught at the Warsaw school of the theatre. Ryszard Cieślak, star of the Grotowski theatre, may serve as an example of the effects achieved by the new training methods. He gave a memorable performance in the title role of *The Constant Prince* and was voted the best foreign actor of the 1960/70 season in New York by American critics after the appearance there of Grotowski's Laboratory Theatre.

The three schools of the theatre in Poland are loca-

ted in Warsaw, Łódź and Cracow. All three are principally interested in training actors although the State
School of the Theatre in Warsaw also has a department
of stage direction. Only graduates of the acting schools
or of other academic institutions in Poland are qualified
to apply. The entrance exams are notably difficult
designed to test not only the applicant's intelligence and
knowledge but also his aptitudes. The Rector of the
State School of the Theatre in Warsaw is the outstanding actor Tadeusz Łomnicki, the dean of the department
of stage direction is Professor Bohdan Korzeniewski.

The state School of the Theatre of Łódź is affiliated
with the Film School. It also offers courses for television
cameramen and directors.

Every school of the theatre has its own theatre where
the students of the acting department are seen in the
graduation plays produced under the guidance of
professors.

Plans are being made for a dramaturgic department to
be organized at the Theatre School of Warsaw. It will
offer courses to drama critics and literary directors of
theatres.

Wrocław has a school for actors of puppet theatres.

CHAPTER VII

THEATRICAL GEOGRAPHY

Directly after the last war there were two important theatrical centres in Poland. These were Łódź and Cracow. The top Polish actors and stage directors congregated in Łódź. This city too had the largest number of theatres. In view of the nearly total devastation of Warsaw, the city could not play the role of the theatrical capital of the country. In 1948 and 1949, the nation's capital made the gigantic effort to make up for lost time and to recapture its leading position in the cultural life of Poland. Leon Schiller moved to Warsaw with a group of the best actors of the Polish Army Theatre of Łódź. Erwin Axer and Michał Melina took the company of the *Kameralny* Theatre of Łódź to the nation's capital and Bronisław Dąbrowski and a number of the leading actors of Cracow joined the Polski Theatre company.

In the years that followed Warsaw held undisputed sway in the life of the Polish theatre. The *Nowy* Theatre of Łódź, where Dejmek was producing plays of bold and sharp political cristicism, represented the only challenge to Warsaw's supremacy. Gradually the Cracow theatres began to achieve prominence; the Katowice theatre had its halcyon days. But it was the Wrocław theatre, with the company of actors it gradually began to form, that rose to first rank among the Polish theatres. The activities of Edmund and Maria Wierciński and Jakub

Rotbaum's brilliant productions were the factors principally responsible for the high rank the Wrocław theatre held in the forties and the fifties.

Important changes occurred on the theatrical map of Poland in 1955—1962. Although Warsaw still held first position in the country, it had lost its preeminent position. Outstanding productions are seen not only in Łódź, Cracow, Wrocław and Katowice, but with a growing frequency in smaller towns where the theatres hold the centre of public attention. The *Ludowy* Theatre established in Nowa Huta in 1955 and headed by Krystyna Skuszanka and Jerzy Krasowski immediately sparked discussions, comments in the press and wide public reaction. Next, the theatre of Zielona Góra, headed by Marek Okopiński and with the valuable cooperation of his literary director Stanisław Hebanowski, became the favourite with the drama critics. An interesting company was shaping up at the *Wybrzeże* Theatre. Here, Zygmunt Hübner first displayed his talent as theatre administrator finding a very good partner in Antoni Biliczak, an unusually gifted organizer and business manager. Jerzy Goliński succeeded Hübner in Gdańsk, continuing his fine work in the theatre. Bydgoszcz, Toruń and Szczecin, as well as other cities, became active theatre centres at this time.

The wide distribution of theatres made it virtually impossible to see all the worthwhile performances. The danger that some of them will remain unnoticed increased. The Drama Critics' Club of the Polish Journalist Association began to organize field trips. In 1959 Hugon Moryciński, director of the theatres of Bydgoszcz and Toruń, proposed a Theatre Festival of Northern Poland. The suggestion was adopted and a festival of the theatres of Białystok, Olsztyn, Gdańsk, Bydgoszcz and Toruń, Grudziądz, Koszalin and Szczecin was organized. The idea behind the festival was to present an annual review and confrontation of the theatres of that region, with the best productions presented to a forum of critics. Toruń was selected as the site of the Theatre Festival of Northern Poland. This old city on the Vistula is noted for its remarkable Gothic architecture, a university and an enthusiastic but demanding public with a discerning taste for the arts.

The first Toruń festival, held in 1959, was an unqualified success. The productions presented by the theatres of Northern Poland were interesting on the whole and very popular with the Toruń public and visitors. The Theatre Festival of Northern Poland is now an annual affair and is one of the best regional events of this type in the country.

A year later Kalisz, an old city on the Prosna River, came forth with a similar idea. Kalisz is the home town of the "father of the national theatre" Wojciech Bogusławski. The theatres of Central Poland, notably of the cities of Poznań, Gniezno, Zielona Góra, Lublin, Kielce and Łódź, come together in Kalisz.

The third festival, held in Wrocław, was originally conceived as a regional event. The theatres of Upper and Lower Silesia, the *Ziemia Opolska* Theatre as well as the *Ziemia Lubuska* Theatre from Zielona Góra were to meet here. But it soon became clear that the Wrocław public were not attracted by this type of festival. They were used to their own very good theatre. Consequently, the Wrocław Festival began to shift its emphasis to finally become a review of Polish contemporary drama.

Rzeszów is the site of theatre encounters where

Cracow, Katowice, Wrocław, Kielce, Lublin and Rze-szów and at times smaller towns of Cracow, Katowice and Wrocław provinces present their productions. Thus, the annual reviews are representative of the work of all the theatres of the country. Held in May and June each year they offer the opportunity to make a fairly accurate judgement of the achievements and weaknesses of the theatres in Poland.

The Drama Critics' Club brought forth the idea of organizing an annual review of the best productions in the country. The idea was finally realized in 1965. That date marked the First Warsaw Theatre Encounter which is now being held every year. The best productions of the year are presented on this occasion. In 1970, for the first time, the event was accompanied by a sym-posium organized by the Drama Critics' Club, devoted to the problems of the theatre in People's Poland. Experts on the theatre, critics, actors, stage directors, stage designers and theatre historians participated in the event.

Hotly discussed in the sixties was the question of the selection of productions seen at the regional festivals and the question of prizes. Some opted for a working session which fact presumed that all the submitted productions should be seen and that no prizes should be awarded. Opponents of this view believed that the festival should be a festive event and demanded that weak or bad productions should be eliminated, that only above average production should be admitted and that prizes should be awarded. The view that a selection of productions should be made and that the regional festivals should be competitive, hence that prizes and citations should be awarded, is gaining the upper hand. Prizes are awarded at the Toruń and Kalisz festivals and recently also in Wrocław. Rzeszów does not award prizes, a fact which diminishes the popularity of this festival. Nor are prizes awarded at the Warsaw Theatre Encounters, but admission to the festival is a prize in itself.

The regional festivals and the Warsaw Theatre Encounters aside, there are also thematic festivals held in Poland. The first of these held in 1947 was the Shakespearean festival. The First Festival of Russian and Soviet Plays was held in 1949 and many years later the idea was taken up by Katowice, which organized a festival of this kind for the theatres of its province and later of the country. The festival is held once every two years or even less frequently. The first festival of plays from the countries of the People's Democracies, which ended in Katowice, was held in 1971. Other nationwide events now are the Wrocław Festival of Contemporary Polish Plays and the Festival of the Theatres of One Actor, organized by the Piwnica Świdnicka Socialist Youth Union Club. The festival of the theatre of miniature forms, that is of studio theatres, is held each year at the Thirteen Muses Club of Szczecin. A television festival of dramatic theatres is organized every year as well.

There were 58 theatre companies with 79 stages operating in Poland in 1970. One of the number is the Yiddish language theatre (in 1970 it received a modern theatre, with a fine auditorium and the latest in stage machinery, which is located in the building of the Jewish Cultural Society in Poland in Warsaw). There is one Pantomime Theatre, 20 lyrical stages (8 operas and 12 operettas), 23 independent puppet theatres and two puppet theatres affiliated with dramatic theatres. Forty cities, some of these with a population of less than 50 thousand have resident companies. A large number of theatres go on tour playing in the small towns and villages of their region. The larger cultural centres of the country have more than one theatre. Warsaw has 21 in all, Cracow and Łódź have 9 each, Wrocław has 7, Poznań — 6 and Katowice and Szczecin — 4 each. There are experimental theatres as well as a large number of cabaret and vaudeville theatres.

The theatrical geography of the country has not changed substantially for many years. Warsaw is still the capital of the theatre with Cracow and Wrocław as its strongest rivals. The theatres of Łódź have not done as outstanding work in the last couple of years. On the other hand, however, the *Wybrzeże* Theatre as well as the theatres of Toruń, Szczecin, Katowice, Bydgoszcz and Olsztyn are doing very interesting work. Izabella Cywińska, director of the Kalisz theatre, has decided to create an avant-garde theatre of young artists. She has attracted the most gifted of the country's young directors Maciej Prus and Helmut Kajzar.

The Polish Theatre and Film Artists Association has a membership of 2,310, the Stage Design Section of the Polish Artists' Union — 154 members, the Drama Critics' Club of the Polish Journalist Association — 112 members and the Polish Section of the International Theatre Institute — 149 artists and critics.

CHAPTER VIII

EXPERIMENTS
AND EXPLORATIONS

Next to the mainstream of theatre life in Poland, there have sprung up in the fifties and sixties a number of subsidiary forms of the performing arts which were not without influence upon the activity of the first theatres of the land. The most important effect was exerted by the student theatre movement.

Two student theatres, the *Bim-Bom* in Gdańsk and the Student Satirical Theatre in Warsaw, founded in 1954, were to set the tone of the whole movement for many years to come. The first STS (as the Student Satirical Theatre is called) programme opened on May 2nd, 1954 under the significant title of *To idzie młodość* (Here Comes Youth). The first programme of *Bim-Bom*, called *Radość poważna* (Serious Joy), set the mood for that theatre's activity. The theatres represented different style and subscribed to different artistic programmes. The STS concentrated principally on political satire of a clear ideological bent. It congregated a group of members of the Polish Youth Union who desired reform of the Republic. The Programmes they put on were closely related in style and mood to the satire of Mayakovsky and the work of Brecht. The purpose was agitation. The following titles reflect the theatre's interests: *Myślenie ma kolosalną przyszłość* (Thinking Has a Colossal Future), *Czarna przegrywa — czerwona wygrywa* (Black Loses — Red Wins), *Agitka,*

Siódmy kolor czerwieni (The Seventh Colour of Red) and *Idź na spacer alegorio* (Take a Walk Allegory). The young people were rationalists and wished to speak without recourse to metaphor about the things that rankled them and that they did not find to their liking in the preceding period in Poland. The majority were young communists.

They were less interested in staging effects and the visual side of the performance, focusing attention wholly on the text and its interpretation. The STS had a group of highly talented writers all of whom later turned to writing contemporary drama. Thus, there was Jarosław Abramow and Andrzej Jarecki, then Agnieszka Osiecka the best lyricist of popular songs and musicals, Ziemowit Fedecki, Witold Dąbrowski, Tadeusz Strumff, Józef Waczkow and others. The stage directors of most of the programmes were Jerzy Markuszewski (he later studied stage directing at the Theatre School) and Wojciech Solarz (who later became film director). But apart from these two, Konrad Swinarski also directed at the STS. The sets were designed by Zofia Góralczyk, the music was composed by Marek Lusztig and Edward Pałłasz. Many of the now famous stars of the Polish stage got their first chance at the STS. In later years celebrated actors of the professional stage appeared at the STS, notably Wojciech Siemion *(Wieża malowana* — The Painted Tower — with text compiled by Ernest Bryll), Alina Janowska *(Oskarżeni* — The Accused), Kalina Jędrusik *(Taboo* according to Jacek Bocheński), Halina Mikołajska *(Letters of Mlle de Lespinasse)*, Andrzej Łapicki *(Sposób bycia* — A Manner of Being (according to Kazimierz Brandys) and others. Toward the end of the sixties, the STS bacame a permanent company subsidized by the People's Council of the nation's capital. The art director is the theatre's founder Andrzej Jarecki. Contact with students insures a steady flow of young talents to the theatre.

Bim-Bom was totally different in character and had a much shorter life. It was organized on the basis of cooperation between professional actors of the *Wybrzeże* Theatre and art students. The founders were two talented young stage actors Zbigniew Cybulski and Bogumił Kobiela. They worked with Jerzy Afanasjew (young satirist, later a film director), Jacek Fedorowicz (who was to become the favourite star of entertainment and most popular television master of ceremonies in Poland), Wowo Bielicki (now a stage designer) and others. The single distinctive feature of the *Bim-Bom* was its poetic style. It did not speak straight out about the important questions of our day but in the form of poetic metaphor, lyrical figures of speech, allegory and allusion. The visual side, the sets and colour, played a far more important part here than in the STS. Students of the Sopot art school, one of the most important art academies in Poland at the time, as well as students of the Polytechnic of Gdańsk, played a fairly large role in the theatre.

The dominant role played by artists in the student theatre of the Coast was to exercise an influence on the activities of other theatres set up on the Coast. The *To Tu* (Here) Theatre was established in 1958, with Wowo Bielicki as stage director, with song lyrics by Jerzy Afanasjew and Jacek Fedorowicz among others and with Tadeusz Chyła, who later won popularity in all of Poland, as a balladeer. The art School of Gdańsk organized the hand pantomime theatre *Co To* (What's That?) based on the same principle as the puppet

140

theatre, in that instead of dolls we had only the hands of the actors. The song lyrics were written by Jerzy Afanasjew. In 1958 he founded the Afanasjew Family Circus where he was joined by his wife Alina Ronczewska-Afanasjew and her brother Ryszard Ronczewski. The most popular programmes put on by the Circus were: *Tralabomba, Białe zwierzęta* (White Animals) and *Dobry wieczór, blaźnie* (Good Evening, Clown). The theatre was distinguished for the sets and visual effects as well as for its abstract humour — very much in the style of the theatre of the absurd. The next student theatre to be established in Gdańsk was descended in a straight line from the Circus. Jerzy Krechowicz's *Galeria* Theatre gave complete precedence to the plastic arts over the text.

Some years after the founding of the STS, the *Hybrydy* was established in Warsaw. The student club, for that's what it was, organized a theatre whose principal purpose and aim was to stimulate young Polish playwrights. Dramatists Janusz Krasiński, Stanisław Grochowiak and others made their debuts here. Such talented authors as Jan Pietrzak, Jonasz Kofta and Adam Kreczmar wrote their first lyrics here.

Łódź had two interesting student theatres active in the fifties and the sixties. *The Pstrąg* (The Trout) had Jan Skotnicki as stage director and *The Cytryna* (The Lemon) had Jan Kwapisz. The theatres maintained lively contact with the literary circle of Łódź (Bogdan Drozdowski, Igor Sikirycki, Tadeusz Gicgier) as well as with young Łódź actors and students of the Łódź Theatre and Film School.

The *Kalambur* (The Pun) student theatre was set up in Wrocław in the sixties. It was first directed by Bogusław Litwiniec and later by Włodzimierz Herman.

The *Kalambur* sought to make use of the experiences of the STS and *Bim-Bom* theatres. Emphasis was placed on the literary texts. The theatre turned to the obscure, though by no means inferior works of Polish literature, although problems of staging and stage design received much attention. The *Kalambur's* biggest hit was the production of *Szewcy* (The Cobblers) by Stanisław Ignacy Witkiewicz, followed by a poetic programme called *Futurystykon* devoted to the avant-garde poetry of the twenties. Another noteworthy programme was *W rytmie słońca* (In the Rythm of the Sun) based on an epic poem by Urszula Kozioł, a young Wrocław poetess.

Cracow became the fourth important centre of student theatres in Poland. The *Teatr 38*, with its moving spirit Waldemar Krygier, was active in Cracow from 1956; Helmut Kajzar made the first steps of his career in this city. Waldemar Krygier played an important part in formulating the programme of the Grotowski theatre while Helmut Kajzar is a rising young dramatist and stage director in the professional theatre. The *Teatr 38* set out to put to a new test the classics of drama and modern Polish and other plays. There was much misunderstanding and extravagance as well as many genuinely successful experiments. The theatre produced Beckett's *Waiting for Godot* and *Endgame* (the world première of latter it is presumed, held on November 14th, 1957), de Ghelderode's *Christopher Columbus,* Dante's *The Divine Comedy* and Krasiński's *Undivine Comedy,* Adamov's *Professor Taranne* and Genet's *The Maids,* Słowacki's *Samuel Zborowski,* Yesenin's *Confessions of a Hoodlum,* Ionesco's *Amédée or How to Get Rid of It,* Borchert's *At the Door,* Chekhov's *Platonov,* Kafka's *Letters to*

Milena, Oedipus Rex by Sophocles. Other productions were *23 Pages of Manuscript* according to Mayakovsky, Strindberg's *Ghost Sonata,* Zapolska's *Morality of Mrs. Dulska, The Mad Locomotive* by Witkiewicz and *The Tragedy of Richard III* according to Shakespeare. Respected classical works were torn apart, turned inside out and given new interpretations. The texts provided an excuse for theatrical games and true creative effort.

The Student University Theatre was established in Cracow later. The best productions were Gogol's *Memoir of a Madman* and *The Fall* according to Różewicz. The theatre produced the talented young stage director Jan Łukowski who, together with his friends, established the "Proscenium" studio theatre as an affilliate of the *Rozmaitości* Theatre. He lived long enough to direct Gogol's *The Nose* and *Salt of Attica* according to Aristophanes. He died in an automobile accident. The gifted director Krzysztof Jasiński also got a start at the theatre.

The *Gong 2* Theatre of Lublin, under the management of Andrzej Rozhin for a number of years, did some notable work. His best productions were *Brecht's Songs* and *Wietnam ukrzyżowany* (Vietnam Crucified). Rozhin is to be soon graduated from the School of the Theatre of Warsaw and is already directing in the professional theatre.

Student theatres prospered in Poznań, Szczecin and in other academic centres of the country. The *Gest* pantomime student theatre of Wrocław is modelled after the Tomaszewski Pantomime Theatre of the same city. A similar student theatre is operating in Szczecin.

The Polish Student Association offers its patronage to the student theatres. The Association organizes annual review and regional and national festivals.

Polish student theatres take part in international student theatre festivals in Nancy, Parma, Erlangen and Zagreb. The International Festival of Student Theatre Festivals, held in Wrocław since 1967, represents very high artistic standards and ranks high among the international student festivals.

The student theatres of Poland not only contributed to the artistic development, not only did they breathe fresh life into the Polish theatre but also produced a cadre of young stage directors.

The satirical cabaret entitled *Koń* (The Horse), the first programme presented in 1957, was born in an atmosphere very much like that of the student theatres. The satirical programme was prepared by the students of the Warsaw School of the Theatre. When they graduated and found themselves at the *Dramatyczny* Theatre of Warsaw, they suggested that the programme be included in the theatre repertory. Thus, it came about that we owe to the decision of Director Meller one of the funniest and wittiest programmes of the whole past 25 years. The cast was composed of the highly talented young actors with clear comic talent who were later hailed the best comedians of the Polish theatre. They were: Mieczysław Czechowicz, Wiesław Gołas, Zbigniew Bogdański, Zdzisław Leśniak and Jerzy Dobrowolski. Nearly all of them were also authors of the text. The programme was a hit. One of the talented young artists, Jerzy Dobrowolski, prepared a satirical programme called *Owca* (The Sheep) many years later which was built along similar lines as *The Horse*.

Wiesław Gołas as Papkin in Fredro's *The Revenge* — caricature by Adam Perzyk

Willeur Goriar

Jestem Poyskim. Lew Tołnocy

Side by side with the spontaneous fun-loving student theatres and similar phenomena, we observe the emergence of the experimental theatre in the fifties and sixties. The experimental theatres were organized and operated primarily by poets and painters. Two of the theatres deserve closer attention: the *Cricot 2* Theatre of Tadeusz Kantor which reverts to the pre-war avant-garde theatre of artists and Miron Białoszewski's *Osobny Theatre* (Separate Theatre) in Warsaw. The *Cricot 2* Theatre was located in the Artist Union Building in Cracow where the *Cricot 1* was located before the war. The difference between the two theatres lay in the fact that the *Cricot 1* placed more emphasis on the literary and political aspects while the *Cricot 2* is above all an avant-garde art theatre interested in artistic experiment. The two finest productions in the history of the theatre were the plays of Witkacy (pen-name of St. I. Witkiewicz) and specifically *Mątwa* (The Cuttlefish) and *The Water Hen,* staged by Kantor. The *Cricot 2* Theatre took part recently in the festival in Nancy. We might note that the famous Cracow artist and stage designer Kazimierz Mikulski works in the theatre.

Miron Białoszewski and Lech Emfazy Stefański ran their *Osobny* Theatre in Białoszewski's apartment at Tarczyńska Street, for which it was at first called. The theatre was short-lived. The programmes consisted of Białoszewski's verses and longer poetic compositions, many of them given very interesting settings. At a time when this type of theatre was still unacclaimed in Europe and in the United States, the little experimental theatres were a rage in Poland, the artists were widely discussed and their work approved or fiercely resisted.

The Grotowski theatre has its roots in the little

experimental theatre. It began with a small group of artists who left Cracow for Opole to found *Teatr 13 Rzędów* (The 13 Row Theatre) where they could experiment with new forms and look for a new approach to the theatre.

It was in 1959 that the Grotowski Theatre held its first première. The play was *Cain* according to Byron. It was followed by *Misterium Buffo* according to Mayakovsky, *Siakuntala* according to Kalidasa, Forefathers' *Eve* according to Mickiewicz, *Kordian* according to Słowacki, *Acropolis* according to Wyspiański and *The Tragical History of Doctor Faustus* according to Marlowe. This last play was seen by members of the Congress of International Theatre Institute (ITI) held in 1963. The participants were greatly impressed. The world press began to write of the Grotowski Theatre in superlatives. In 1965 the Grotowski Laboratory Theatre moved to Wrocław. *The Constant Prince* and *Apocalypsis cum figuris* were the two plays produced here and the theoretical principles of the Laboratory Theatre method were formulated at this stage. We read in the principles of the Laboratory Theatre and its functions: "The aim of the Laboratory Theatre is to examine by way of practical experience the technical and creative problems of the theatre with special attention given to the acting art. The purpose of the analysis is to improve the actor's work in the theatre and to achieve a general development of the acting craft... In addition to these studies, the Laboratory Theatre presents the results of its work in the form of stage productions: the fundamental activity of the theatre is not ordinary public service but research and experimentation. The Laboratory Theatre functions through: a) studies in the area of acting technique with special attention to creative training, b) productions of an experimental acting and staging texture; these are the working models on which the actors test the effects of the elements of technique and training that had been discovered, c) documentation of tested elements of technique by, among others, producing written descriptions of exercises for actors as well as of other elements useful in creating roles, d) instruction for trainees from other theatres and theatrical centres (including foreign centres as well) within the limits of actual needs and the theatre's capabilities."

Grotowski holds to the principle of creating a modest theatre with the actor as the most important and virtually the only element in the production as well as its basic material. There are no stage settings in the theatre. The actors perform in the centre of an empty area with the spectators seated under the walls. There are not more than 34 to 40 persons in an audience. Actors are thus able to establish direct contact with the audience. The Grotowski Theatre acts upon the emotions and probes the human consciousness and subconsciousness. It reverts to the Stanislavsky method, that is, the actors live their part and get into the characters they portray. It is not unaware of Antonin Artaud's experiments and search of the theatre of cruelty. To the Grotowski Theatre the text is no more than a point of departure for the actor and the fabric of the story is a frame of reference for audience imagination. The acting technique of Grotowski's actors is superb. Their gestures and movements assume inordinate eloquence. They exercise their bodies so as to be able to tackle every acting chore. With the "resonator" technique they develop power and control of voice emission and the ability to modulate the volume from a whisper to a shout.

The Grotowski Theatre undertakes problems that beset the contemporary world. Hence, fear of alienation, despair at the hostility of everybody against everybody and at the threat of annihilation, protest against human suffering. This is the character of Grotowski's three most recent productions. *Acropolis* contains an allusion to the extermination camp of Auschwitz, *The Constant Prince* is a tale of man's inexpressible suffering. *Apocalypsis cum figuris* is a modern mystery play of the Lord's Passion.

Ritual plays an important role in the Grotowski Theatre. In its simplicity and exaltation it stands close to medieval art. In the course of the best performances the actors and the audience are drawn into a communion of deep experience and emotion.

The numerous tours across the European continent, appearances in New York and at the Shiraz Festival have spread the fame of the Grotowski Theatre all over the world.

The "Studio" Theatre set up in 1971 in Warsaw under the direction of Józef Szajna is also experimental in character. Grotowski's primary interest is the actor, Szajna's is the stage design and the costume. Szajna's productions, the most important of which so far was *Faust*, put on at the *Polski* Theatre in Warsaw are actually plastic compositions in motion. Actors, robed in strage costumes and arranged in compositions of enormous evocative power, are the material of the staging.

Henryk Tomaszewski's Pantomime Theatre began as a modest little company. Henryk Tomaszewski was a member of the Wrocław ballet. When he found that dancing did not quite fulfil his ambitions he decided to pantomime. In the beginning he too appeared on stage, among others, during the Democratic Youth World Festival held in Warsaw in 1955 where he won one of the main prizes. Though Marcel Marceau made a deep impression on Tomaszewski, he wished to develop something new and not to imitate the great mime. He established a theatre with no soloists or stars. As in the dramatic theatre, but using different techniques, the whole ensemble worked together to interpret literary works on the stage. He used ancient myth, legend, stories and other literary classics and modern works. The production of Gogol's *The Overcoat* brought him his first great success. The early programmes were composed of short and long pantomime scenes although it was clear that Tomaszewski was clearly attracted by full length pantomime plays. *Gilgamesh, Odejście Fausta* (Faust's Departure), *Sen nocy listopadowej* (November Night's Dream) staged beautifully by Tomaszewski, represent the theatre's crowning achievement. The theatre toured Great Britain, the German Federal Republic, the USSR, Spain, Italy and many other countries. The Pantomime Theatre received the Grand Prix at the international ballet festival held in Paris in 1970.

In Poland as well we observe the emergence of a highly original theatre form, known here as the Theatre of One Actor. The rise of the theatre may be ascribed to the desire of actors, who do not have the opportunity to display their talents in the theatres, to find an outlet for their ambitions. In the Theatre of One Actor they may choose texts that interest them and work on them as long as they wish and as is necessary from the artistic point of view. Finally, they are able to appear where and when they find it fitting. It has been proved in practice that this theatre form can count on wide public appeal, that it attracts large numbers of devoted fans and that it can be operated very cheaply, because it requires no large auditoriums and stages or costly sets. The theatre of One Actor can be easily moved to clubs and community houses as well as travel to distant out of the way localities.

The origins of the Theatre of One Actor are connected with the work of Danuta Michałowska, formerly of the *Rapsodyczny* Theatre of Cracow headed by Mieczysław Kotlarczyk. The *Rapsodyczny* devoted itself principally to the interpretation of poetic drama. Michałowska was the first to prove that a single actor on an empty stage can create a genuine theatre. The Theatre of One Actor calls for absolute simplicity and naturalness. The spectators are seated close to the stage and listen to the actor as if he were a guest at their home who wishes to tell them something interesting. Michałowska's idea was quickly picked up by other actors. Many of them, such as Kalina Jędrusik, Wojciech Siemion, Andrzej Łapicki and Halina Mikołajska, appeared in programmes on the stage of the STS theatre in Warsaw. Many others prepared programmes they could take on tours. This theatre form spread most quickly in Cracow. There, next to Danuta Michałowska, we have Irena Jun and Lidia Zamkow, Halina Gryglaszewska, Tadeusz Malak, Jerzy Nowak, Maria Kościałkowska and others. In Cracow as well Ryszard Filipski presented his brilliant programmes, and it is perhaps Filipski who has achieved the epitome of naturalness and simplicity charged with unusual power of expression. With the help of the Cracow City Council's Department of Culture and of the Central Office of the

Socialist Youth Union, Filipski established his own Theatre of One Actor in 1970.

The theatre is located in the cellar of the old Town Hall building. At the inauguration of his theatre, Filipski presented a programme dedicated to the great Polish scholar, rector of the University of Cracow and authority of international law Paweł Włodkowic, (Paulus Vladimir circa 1370—1435).

Through the efforts of the Socialist Youth Union's Working Youth Club, the *"Piwnica Świdnicka"* of Wrocław has been organizing annual Festivals of the Theatre of One Actor since 1965. Among the winners of this unique event are, aside from Ryszard Filipski (for a very interesting adaptation of a reportage. *Co jest za tym murem* (What Is Behind that Wall) by Jacek Stwora, Zofia Rysiówna (for *Życie* (Life) — an adaptation from Ernest Bryll's novel), Halina Gryglaszewska (for a programme about women prisoners of Nazi concentration camps who were used as guinea pigs in the pseudo-scientific experiments), Maria Kościałkowska (for her interpretation of Wyspiański's play *Protesilas and Laodamia)*, Irena Jun (for *Pastorałki góralskie* (Mountain Christmas Carols) by Harasymowicz), Lidia Zamkow (for a programme about Edith Piaf), Tadeusz Malak (for a remarkable interpretation of the prose and verses of Różewicz and the prose of Herbert), Halina Słojewska (for a sensitive rendition of the prose of Bruno Schulz), a Wrocław physician Andrzej Dziedziul (for Hamlet and Faust performed with puppets) and others.

The *Piwnica Świdnicka* Festivals provide incentive to the development of the Theatre of One Actor and promote interest in this theatre form in Wrocław. There, next to Andrzej Dziedziul, the leading actress of the *Polski* Theatre, Anna Lutosławska, and talented actor

Scene from *Arturo Ui* by Berthold Brecht as directed by Erwin Axer. Kazimierz Opaliński as Dogsborough and Tadeusz Łomnicki as Ui at the *Współczesny* Theatre of Warsaw

Mirosława Dubrawska and Władysław Krasnowiecki in Arthur Miller's *Death of a Salesman* at the *Ateneum* in Warsaw

Ryszard Cieślak and Rena Mirecka in *The Constant Prince* by Calderon-Słowacki produced by Jerzy Grotowski at the Laboratory Theatre of Wrocław

Wyspiański's *The Wedding* directed by Adam Hanuszkiewicz and with stage sets by Adam Kilian

A Midsummer Night's Dream by Shakespeare at the *Polski* Theatre in Poznań. Crowd Scene

Ulysses by Joyce in an adaptation by Maciej Słomczyński, directed by Zygmunt Hübner at the *Wybrzeże* Theatre of Gdańsk

Stanisław Igar as Bloom

Daniel Olbrychski as Hamlet and Zofia Kucówna as Gertrude
in the *Narodowy* Theatre production of *Hamlet*. Direction
Adam Hanuszkiewicz, stage sets by Marian Kołodziej

of the *Współczesny* Theatre, Edward Lubaszenko, have done extremely fine work in this form.

The one actor theatre form and the movement of the theatre of miniature forms is flourishing not only in Cracow, Warsaw, Wrocław, and Poznań but also in other, some of them smaller, centres. For example, a young student of the Cracow School of the Theatre, Elżbieta Fediuk, appeared in Wrocław in 1970 in a programme that appealed to the public. There are already stage directors who devote themselves to this form of the theatre. Foremost among these is Lidia Żukowska of Cracow. She provided guidance and advice to Ryszard Filipski in his first programmes and in 1970 prepared Lidia Zamkow's new programme. The centre of the theatre of miniature forms is Szczecin with its *Klub 13 Muz* and the *Krypta*. The productions use a larger cast but the principles of organization, the plays put on and the rehearsals recall by the method employed the Theatre of One Actor. The Annual Festival of the Theatre of Miniature Forms held in Szczecin admits both the Theatres of One Actor as well as productions with a larger cast. Studio theatres are springing up in many Polish cities, many of them affiliated with the large theatres or actually a part of these in the financial and organizational sense (like the theatre in the round of the *Ateneum* or the Rehearsal Theatre of the *Dramatyczny* Theatre of Warsaw and the recently opened *Reduta 70* of the Lublin theatre and others).

The mammoth outdoor entertainments provide a contrast to the miniature theatre forms. These too enjoy great popularity among the Polish audiences. The sight and sound spectaculars are presented in the fabulous Renaissance courtyard of the royal castle at Wawel in Cracow. Before the war the courtyard served as the setting for *The Dismissal of the Greek Envoys* by Jan Kochanowski and for Calderon's *The Constant Prince* in an adaptation by Słowacki. After the war Bronisław Dąbrowski directed a very successful production of Shakespeare's *Twelfth Night* at the castle. Another tradition was established by Juliusz Osterwa in the interwar years. He and the *Reduta* company gave performances in the small cities and towns, some of these played against the beautiful old setting of period architecture. The Osterwa Theatre of Lublin reverts to this tradition today when it gives performances in the old town settings of its region (as in Kazimierz on the Vistula) and outdoor productions of Shakespeare (*Romeo and Juliet*). The Rzeszów Theatre has performed *Hamlet* and *Le Cid* in the courtyard of the Renaissance castle of Baranów. One of the most striking performances of Shakespeare's plays was given by the *Wybrzeże* Theatre in the courtyard of the gloomy Teutonic castle of Malbork. The play fittingly was *Macbeth*. There are many lovely outdoor settings found in Poznań and Kalisz and their environs, to mention the memorable performance at Gołuchów castle. The region of Kielce as well offers a large number of opportunities in this area. There is the square in front of the Bishop's Castle in the capital of the province as well as many lovely settings in historical Sandomierz and other old towns of the province.

Finally the Polish cabaret, one of the theatre forms with the Polish public. The traditions go back to the early 20th century when Tadeusz Boy Żeleński and his friends transplanted the model of the *Chat Noir* of Paris to Poland. The first excellent Polish cabaret set up at the time was called *Zielony Balonik* (The Green Balloon). It was located in Cracow in a café which is now known as *Jama Michalikowa*. One may still see on the walls of the café pictures painted by the leading Polish Modernists and the puppets of the cabaret displayed in the cases. Since Cracow is a city that venerates tradition, the *Jama Michalikowa* cabaret was founded by the writers and actors of Cracow in the very same café in the late fifties.

The *Dudek* cabaret at the Nowy Świat Café, headed by Edward Dziewoński, has been operating in Warsaw for some years. Equally famous are the cabarets *Owca* (The Sheep), *Pod Egidą* (At the Aegis), run by Pietrzak, Kofta and Kreczmar, *Pod Kandelabrami, Złoty Kłos* (The Gold Stalk) and others. Literary cabarets operated in Łódź, Wrocław (*Dreptak*) and in other Polish cities.

This in brief is the pictures of paratheatrical phenomena in Poland.

CHAPTER IX

THEATRICAL GRASS-ROOTS

The Polish theatre today is not only what happens on stage and backstage but also includes the area on the other side of the ramp: audience reaction to the plays and the mass movement that flourished in the realm of Melpomene, the beautiful muse of the theatre. The developments noted in Poland after the war have stimulated the development of the professional theatre.

The first of these is the amateur theatre movement. It has a long tradition of over 60 years in Poland and distinct organizational forms. The movement originated in the southern Little Poland region. The theatre was an important factor in reawakening national, political and civic consciousness among the rural population. It was closely bound with the peasant movement and the peasant universities of the period before the last world war. Not only peasant and civic leaders, like Jędrzej Czerniak and Ignacy Solarz, were involved in the movement but also progressive writers like Leon Kruczkowski and Adam Polewka. After 1945 the movement concentrated its activity on the theatre, on developing theatre appreciation. Thus, the rural area of Poland was exposed to the theatre long before television reached it. The amateur theatre movement also inspired greater interest in the professional theatre .

Thousands of amateur theatres are active in Polish towns and villages today. The central agency is the

Amateur Theatre Union with departments in provinces and counties. It provides theatre training, lends costumes, provides advice in matters of art and publishes a journal called *Scena* which brings interesting articles about the professional and amateur theatre as well as information on the repertory and plays suitable for the amateur theatre. The Union organizes an annual competition, called "Closer to the Theatre." Its purpose is to strengthen the ties between the amateur movement and the professional theatre and to stimulate initiatives that would realize this programme. Awards are conferred to the provinces, groups, individuals and professional companies which organized the largest number of events, discussions and meetings whose purpose is to bring the audiences and the theatres closer together. The Union also takes an active part in contests for readers and similar undertakings aimed at arousing interest in the stage.

Community houses and civic centres operate under the patronage of the Ministry of Culture and Art, "Ruch" and other institutions and civic organizations. The Central Counciling Agency of the Amateur Artistic Movement of the Ministry of Culture and Art was in charge of this activity for many years.

In later years, amateur groups began to flourish in the working-class communities and among the youth. A number of very good amateur groups were active in the factory culture and recreation clubs organized by trade unions. Reviews and festivals held periodically bring attention to very interesting artistic work. The amateur theatre movement is also doing very well in schools of every level and in youth organizations, such as the Rural Youth Union, Socialist Youth Union, the

Polish Pathfinders, the Polish Student Association and others.

In addition to the amateur movement a new development has been observed in the sixties: the theatre fan club movement. Here, we have people who do not wish to do anything in the theatre but who would like to know more about it, take part in discussions about the theatre and come into closer contact with theatre artists. They are the backbone of the professional theatre's survival, being the most loyal audience and fans insuring good attendance and creating a friendly and warm atmosphere for the artists. Fan clubs are distributed throughout the country. There are more than one thousand of these. The most active and the largest number of clubs are in Cracow. Hundreds of these clubs are active among the intellectuals, workers and youth. The membership totals over 25 thousand. Greatest emphasis is placed on schoolclubs in Cracow. They organize weekly discussions on plays currently seen in the theatres to which the artists are invited, lectures on the history and theory of the theatre, information about the most important events in the theatre and others. Courses on the theatre are offered to teachers who are in charge of the school theatre fan clubs and a kind of university course for all who are interested in the theatre. Members attend rehearsals and dress rehearsal and are entitled to discounts on theatre tickets. In cooperation with the daily *Dziennik Polski*, the clubs organize an annual poll for the best production of the year and the best popular actor. Similar clubs are found in Łódź, Wrocław, Gdańsk and other important cultural centres of the country. Fan clubs are sometimes organized in the small towns and settlements as well.

Not all the communities that have theatre fan clubs have their own professional theatre. But the television reaches everyone offering people the opportunity to see plays transmitted by that medium. The friends of the TV theatre club movement has been gaining force in Poland in recent years. The sponsors are the weekly *Tygodnik Kulturalny* and the Popular Knowledge Society. There are one thousand TV Theatre Fan Clubs in Poland today.

The fan clubs are beginning to work closer with the amateur movement. This leads to the integration of the mass theatre movement. The amateur theatres either merge with theatre fan clubs or simply take over these clubs.

The activity of the theatre fan clubs is coordinated by the Theatre Fan Club Council. In March 1971 the two movements were integrated into one mass theatre movement and took the name of the Theatrical Culture Association.

The International Theatre Day, initiated by the International Theatre Institute, was observed in Poland with great pomp and ceremony. It became an occasion for a holiday of the theatre mass movement. Congresses, sessions and symposium for theatre audiences were held on this day devoted to current theatre problems and reactions to it, actors and stage directors were invited to meet the audience and results of theatre polls were announced, favourite actors received prizes, certificates and flowers and so on.

There is a growing interest in the theatre among Polish youth. Not only are there theatre fan clubs in the schools, not only do students attend the theatre regularly but courses on the theatre are being gradually introduced into the school curriculum. In some of the larger cities, such as Wrocław and Cracow, schools organize in cooperation with the theatre contests for reviews of performances written by the students. The students often come up with refreshingly original observations, testifying to the fact that young Poles are getting to understand the theatre and to react to it with increasing sensitivity. Some of the reviews were published in the theatre journals and specialistic publications. *Filipinka*, a journal for young girls, also prints observations on the theatre submitted by young readers.

CHAPTER X

TELEVISION AND RADIO THEATRE

Although the live theatre has a large audience and devoted fans yet it is the television theatre of Poland which has the widest circle of viewers. At the beginning of 1971 about four or five new plays were transmitted each week by the two television theatre programmes. Thus, there was a television play on the air nearly every day of the week. Some of the programmes are replayed after a certain lapse of time, others are shown interchangeable on programmes I and II. The television theatre will grow in popularity when colour television comes in. Poland will have colour television toward the end of 1973 according to present estimates. At present, about ten million viewers watch the TV television programmes.

The Monday television theatre programmes are perhaps the most popular. That is the television theatre day in Poland. On that day, nearly all the dramatic theatres are closed, the actors have the evening off and theatregoers are at home and so able to watch the television programme. The Monday night theatre presents original productions of new plays, all as a rule of the highest artistic quality. The programme offers classics of Polish and world literature as well as the best Polish and other contemporary plays. Occasionally, the theatre presents plays written especially for the television medium. The plays are directed by prominent

Polish stage directors of the older and younger generation.

By its specific nature, the television theatre comes closer to the theatre than to the film, although the best directors seek to develop an original television form. Perhaps most successful in this effort was Adam Hanuszkiewicz, for many years head of the Polish television theatre. He later put to use in the dramatic theatre the experience gained at the TV studios. Hanuszkiewicz now heads the *Narodowy* Theatre of Warsaw. It was he who first discovered that poetic texts are ideally suited to the TV medium. The most recent example of this kind of television presentation was the very beautiful version of *Pan Tadeusz* by Adam Mickiewicz.

Another outstanding director who found an outlet for his talent in the television is Jerzy Antczak, currently programme director of the television theatre. Although he seems to feel best in the film convention, Antczak, came to the television theatre from the theatre. He is at his best in staging plays based on documentary material, where fiction is molded harmoniously with an authentic background and historical events. Notable among these were the plays on which Antczak collaborated with Zdzisław Skowroński, a remarkable scenario writer who died in 1969. With Skowroński he produced the now famous play, called *Maestro*, which received the Prix Italia. After Skowroński's death Antczak worked alone on scripts for the plays and montages of fact he directed. The most successful was *Epilog norymberski* (The Nuremberg Epilogue), an account of the trial of Nazi criminals in 1945. But Antczak did well in straight theatre, winning the Grand Prix at the Bled

Festival, held in 1970, for his staging of *Uncle Vanya* in Yugoslavia.

Aside from the Monday night theatre, the Polish television presents a variety of other plays and spectacles. Every Thursday, there is the programme of the Mystery and Science Fiction Theatre, Friday — plays presented by regional studios, Saturday — entertainment programmes.

An interesting innovation is a programme called the Prose Theatre which presents adaptations of masterpieces of world literature. Among the adaptations seen in the series were: Martin du Gard's *The Thibault Family*, Sholokhov's *How Quiet Flows the Don*, Mann's *The Buddenbrooks*, *Homo Faber* by Frisch, *The Adventures of the Good Soldier Schweik* by Hašek as well as television adaptations of Polish novels: Dąbrowska's *Bogumił and Barbara*, *Sława i chwała* (Fame and Glory) by Iwaszkiewicz, *Popioły* (Ashes) by Żeromski, *Emancypantki* (The Suffragettes) by Prus and Breza's *The Bronze Gate*. Then there is the Theatre of Fact. *The Nuremberg Epilogue* and the documentary montages about Churchill and Sikorski may be included in this category.

The monodrama, an equivalent of the Theatre of One Actor, is also presented on television. Seen in the programme are often adaptations of presentations which have enjoyed success on the stages of many cities. Thus, the monologues by Ryszard Filipski, Halina Gryglaszewska, Wojciech Siemion and others. The student theatre as well as the poetry theatre and the Literary Theatre are fitted into the television programmes. The series includes programmes devoted to Polish and other poetry.

The Television Theatre Encounters, organized with

the cooperation of Friends of the TV Theatre Clubs, and theatre fan clubs, correspond to the friends of the theatre movement. The plays shown in the programme are grouped in series according to theme. Hence, early and contemporary comedy, the Shakespearean drama, the Soviet revolutionary drama and others. The programme is scheduled for Sunday afternoon. The most interesting letters from readers are read before each programme. Discussions held after the play are attended by the most active fans of the TV theatre, invited to the studio.

The TV theatre in Poland also introduces its viewers to the best TV theatre productions in the world. The best television plays which won awards or were presented at international festivals as well as programmes devoted to the great artists of the contemporary theatre are televised once every month.

The Polish TV theatre programmes were at first transmitted live from the studios. This was before the necessary technical apparatus was available. The effects were very good for there was a sense of tension and suspense now missing which always accompanies the birth of something new. The performances were later taped but the results were mediocre due to the inferior quality of the recording. Now a large proportion of the Polish TV plays are recorded on ampex. Though technically the results are much better yet purists might feel that from the point of view of the principle of the theatre this may not be quite the thing to do. It might be that a return to live transmission would be to the purpose and desirable for the majority of the television plays.

The Polish television theatre, one may make bold to state, has developed its own original style and methods

Helena Chamiecka as Agafia in Gogol's *Marriage* — caricature by Edward Głowacki

which distinguish it both from the theatre and from the film. Every summer the television organizes the Festival of Dramatic Theatres. The plays presented during the summer vacation (when most of the theatres are closed) include productions of the best regional theatres that were singled out for excellence in the regional festivals or that received high critical praise. But the productions are effective only when the specific nature and demands of the medium are taken into account and when they are adapted for the television.

Work of the highest quality is turned in by Adam Hanuszkiewicz, Jerzy Antczak, Jerzy Gruza, Olga Lipińska and a few other TV theatre directors who have become specialized in the field as well as by set designer Xymena Zaniewska who has been collaborating with the television theatre for years and become an expert in her profession. Their efforts prove that the TV theatre may be and is in many cases a separate and original form of creative effort.

The Polish Radio Theatre is fifty years old. For a half century now, the radio has been broadcasting programmes written especially for the "theatre of the imagination" or based on adaptations of stage plays and literary prose. The Polish Radio Theatre has to its credit a number of adaptations of Polish and world literary masterpieces as well as interesting programmes based on contemporary literature. Programmes for children and young listeners constitute an interesting feature of the Polish Radio Theatre's activity.

The Polish Radio Theatre offers excellent training and experience for dramatists. This is where they perfect their skill in writing dialogue. Not by chance did the master of stage dialogue Jerzy Szaniawski, author of the classic in radio dramas *Zegarek* (The Watch) start in the Polish Radio Theatre. A whole group of young Polish dramatists graduated from the radio theatre school. They are Janusz Krasiński, Jarosław Abramow and Stanisław Grochowiak.

One of the great services rendered by the Polish Radio Theatre is the recording of voices of great actors. The tapes may be replayed many years after their death. Stefan Jaracz as well as Aleksander Zelwerowicz liked to appear in the radio plays. All Polish actors willingly take part in the productions of the Polish Radio Theatre for it gives them a remarkable chance to polish their delivery. The word, the actor's voice, becomes the sole tool of the artist. He must build character by voice alone without the help of sets, costumes, props, gestures, facial expression. The radio calls for maximum concentration and enormous intellectual and emotional effort on the part of the actor. He must communicate by word alone, create an evocative picture and mood and prod the listener's imagination by the inflection of his voice. This training may come useful to actors when they face the audience on the stage or the television cameras.

The radio play director is a specialist in his field. He must have a sensitive ear to every tone and intonation and concentrate on directing dialogue.

Poland's most famous radio theatre directors are Zbigniew Kopalko, Wojciech Maciejowski, Edward Pła-czek and Natalia Szydłowska.

CHAPTER XI

DRAMA CRITICISM

Drama criticism has a long and laudable tradition in Poland. Its role was more important in Poland than in many other countries. In the period of Poland's partition the censorship of the occupying powers did not permit writing about many problems of the country. Drama criticism then became the field of activity of publicists who under the guise of discussing a stage drama expressed views not only on the subject of art but also on issues relating to the nation and its life. Consequently, many editors-in-chief of newspapers devoted themselves to drama criticism. A good deal of newspaper space was given over to articles on the theatre. Readers grew accustomed to this editorial form and it was popular with them. The most famous tradition of Polish drama criticism goes back to the *Iksy group* of anonymous authors who wrote remarkable reviews in the first half of the 19th century signing themselves with the pseudonym Iks. In the second half of the 19th century, Władysław Bogusławski, well known Warsaw critic, won a highly reputable positon in the area. He was succeeded at the turn of this century by Jan Lorentowicz. Both men were directors of Warsaw theatres for a while. The brilliant director of the Cracow theatre, Stanisław Koźmian, and the reformer of that theatre, Tadeusz Pawlikowski, began their activity as drama critics. Finally, Leon Schiller began his career with reviews or actually essays on the theatre.

In the years between the two wars, the leading drama critic in Poland was the celebrated author and publicist Tadeusz Boy-Żeleński. He was a poet, satirist, literary historian and outstanding authority and translator of French literature (particularly of the works of Balzac and Proust). His articles on the theatre are marked by erudition and expertise on literature and the theatre. They still provide excellent reading today. Another noted critic at the time was Karol Irzykowski, a man with an education in philosophy and German literature. His reviews were noted for precise philosophical analysis.

After 1945 as theatres sprang up in all part of the country drama criticism flourished. The major papers of large cities and provincial journals devoted a good deal of attention to the theatres. Nearly every production received coverage in the daily newspapers. Some of the journals carried reviews and information about the theatre, conducted campaigns and organized events and theatre polls. The *Dziennik Polski* of Cracow sponsored the Friends of the Theatre Club and organized an annual popularity poll of Cracow actors; *Express Wieczorny* of Warsaw organized recitals of well known actors in the suburbs of the city and awarded the "Golden Mask" to the most popular TV actor or actress chosen by popular vote, *Kurier Polski* of Warsaw sponsored a programme every season called "To the Theatre with the Kurier."

Three types of drama criticism developed in Poland. The first included reviews and essays on the theatre printed in the daily papers. These are short pieces and do not concern themselves with theatre analysis (some theatre artists resent this). These reviews are designed for the general reader and are addressed to those who have not seen or will never see the play. The purpose and aim is to give an evaluation of the production, to describe its good and bad qualities. Leading representatives of this type of review are: August Grodzicki whose reviews are carried by *Życie Warszawy*, Jan Alfred Szczepański (Jaszcz) who writes for *Trybuna Ludu* and the undersigned who is also a reviewer on that paper.

The second category of drama criticism in Poland is the literary essay published in weeklies and literary journals. Here the writers are concerned with problems of the drama and stage presentation and their reactions to them. These articles are usually of fine literary quality. Jan Kott wrote this type of review over many years for the literary journal *Przegląd Kulturalny*. A large proportion of his articles later were included in his book on Shakespeare. The book has had many translations. Other critics in this group are: Jerzy Koenig and Jan Kłossowicz who write for *Współczesność*; Zygmunt Greń and Jan Paweł Gawlik (now director of the *Stary* Theatre of Cracow) whose articles appear in *Życie Literackie* of Cracow; Witold Filler and Wojciech Natanson writing in *Kultura* of Warsaw, Józef Keler at *Odra* issued in Wrocław and Michał Misiorny in the *Litery* of Gdańsk.

The third category of drama criticism includes theoretical works on the theatre. These appear in *Pamiętnik Teatralny, in Teatr,* a quarterly edited by Jerzy Koenig and in the monthly magazine *Dialog,* edited by Stanisław Stampfl. A leading authority on the theatre in Poland who writes on the contemporary theatre occasionally is Professor Zbigniew Raszewski. Then there is the noted critic and theatre authority Konstanty Puzyna, Dr Stanisław Marczak-Oborski and Associate Professor Stanisław Kaszyński. Polish critics and theorists of the theatre also publish books on the theatre, the Polish and European drama.

Some of the Polish drama critics devote their efforts to popularize the theatre, theatre appreciation, the amateur theatre movement, the friends of the theatre movement, the puppet theatre and others. One of the most interesting authors who concerns himself with theatre appreciation is Andrzej Hausbrandt.

Zenobiusz Strzelecki concerns himself principally with problems of stage design in Poland. He has written two standard works in the field.

Television drama criticism and works on the theatre in television is a fairly new branch in Poland. But it is expected that it will develop in the next few years. *Tygodnik Kulturalny* devotes a good deal of attention to the discussion of television theatre productions.

Aside from *Teatr, Dialog* and *Pamiętnik Teatralny* published in Poland there are also the monthly *Scena,* organ of the mass theatre movement, and *Le Teatre en Pologne,* a journal published in French and English which brings articles and information about the Polish theatre designed for foreign readers. It is published by the International Theatre Institute in Poland.

Polish drama critics are members of the Drama Critics Club of the Polish Journalist Union. The club awards the "Boy Prize" each year for the best theatre production of the year and a prize for the most interesting review, essay and book on the theatre. Some Polish critics are members of the Polish Writers' Union. The Polish Journalist Union's Drama Critics Club belongs to the *Association Internationale des Critiques de Theatre.* In 1969 the chairman of the Drama Critics' Club of the Journalist Union was elected chairman of the international association, a signal expression of appreciation for Polish drama criticism and for the Polish theatre.

BIBLIOGRAPHY

Almanach Sceny Polskiej (Polish Theatre Almanac). The Art and Film Publishers.

Csató, Edward: *Le theatre polonais contemporain* (The Contemporary Polish Theatre). Warsaw 1963.

Csató, Edward: *Les metteurs en scene polonais* (Polish Stage Directors). Warsaw 1963.

Csató, Edward: *Polski teatr współczesny pierwszej połowy wieku XX* (The Contemporary Polish Theatre of the First Half of the 20th Century). Warsaw 1967.

Csató, Edward: *Leon Schiller.* Warsaw 1968.

Grodzicki, August: *Le Theatre* (The Theatre), Warsaw 1956.

Hartmann, Karl: *Das polnische Theater nach den Zweiten Weltkrieg* (The Polish Theatre after the Second World War). Marburg 1964.

Marczak-Oborski, Stanisław: *Teatr czasu wojny 1939—1945* (The Theatre during the War of 1939—1945) Warsaw 1967.

Marczak-Oborski, Stanisław: *Życie teatralne w latach 1944—1964* (Life in the Theatre in 1944—1964). Warsaw 1968.

Misiołek, Edmund: *Bibliographie theatrale polonaise 1944—1964* (Bibliography of the Polish Theatre 1944—1964). Warsaw 1965.

Misiorny, Michał: *Teatry dramatyczne Ziem Zachodnich 1945—1960* (The Dramatic Theatres of the Western Territories 1945—1960). Poznań 1963.

Nowicki, Roman: *Theatre Schools in Poland.* Warsaw 1962.

Strzelecki, Zenobiusz: *Polska plastyka teatralna* (Polish Stage Design). Warsaw 1963.

Szydłowski, Roman: *Brecht en Pologne* (Brecht in Poland). Warsaw 1969.

Teatr w Polsce Współczesnej (The Theatre in Contemporary Poland). Texts and selection of photographs. A. Grodzicki and R. Szydłowski. Introduction by Konstanty Puzyna. Warsaw 1963.

Teatry studenckie w Polsce (Student Theatres in Poland). Warsaw 1968.

MONOGRAPHS ON SPECIAL SUBJECTS

Szczublewski, Józef: *Wielki i smutny teatr warszawski 1868—1880* (The Great and Sad Warsaw Theatre of 1868—1880). Warsaw 1963.

Szczublewski, Józef: *Pierwsza "Reduta" Osterwy* (Osterwa's First Redoubt). Warsaw 1965.

Szczublewski, Józef: *Artyści i urzędnicy czyli szaleństwa Leona Schillera* (Artists and Bureaucrats or the Madness of Leon Schiller). 1961.

Raszewski, Zbigniew: *Staroświecczyzna i postęp czasu* (Obsolescence and the Progress of Time). Warsaw 1963.

Timoszewicz, Jerzy: *"Dziady" w inscenizacji Leona Schillera.* ("Forefathers' Eve" in a Stage Adaptation by Leon Schiller). Warsaw 1970.

MONOGRAPHS AND ALBUMS ON INDIVIDUAL THEATRES

Czanerle, Maria: *Teatr pokolenia* (The Theatre of a Generation). Łódź 1964.

Lipiec, Wanda: *Zelwerowicz i scena łódzka* (Zelwerowicz and the Łódź Theatre). Łódź 1960.

Kaczorowska-Herman, Maria: *Andrzeja Mielewskiego Teatr Popularny w Łodzi* (Andrzej Mielewski's Popularny Theatre of Łódź). 1970.

Kaszyński, Stanisław: *Teatry Łódzkie 1945—1962.* (The Łódź Theatres. 1945—1962). Łódź 1970.

Krasiński, Edward: *Teatr Jaracza* (The Jaracz Theatre). Warsaw 1970.

Olszewski, Kazimierz: *Śląska kronika teatralna 1914—1922* (The Theatre Chronicle of Silesia. 1914—1922). Cracow 1969.

Szczepkowska, Malwina: *20 lat teatru na Wybrzeżu* (20 Years of the Theatre on the Coast). Gdynia 1968.

100 lat Starego Teatru w Krakowie (A Hundred Years of the Stary Theatre of Cracow). Cracow 1965.

75 lat Teatru im. Słowackiego w Krakowie (75 Years of the Słowacki Theatre of Cracow). Cracow 1968.

Teatr Narodowy w Warszawie 1949—1961 (The Narodowy Theatre of Warsaw. 1949—1961). Warsaw 1962.

Teatr Dramatyczny m. st. Warszawy (The Dramatyczny Theatre of the Capital City of Warsaw). Warsaw 1958.

ESSAYS, REVIEWS AND COMMENTARY

Axer, Erwin: *Listy ze sceny* (Letters from the Stage). Warsaw 1965. Second Series. Warsaw 1957.

Axer, Erwin: *Sprawy teatralne* (Theatrical Matters). Warsaw 1966.

Bechczyc-Rudnicka, Maria: *Godziny osobliwe* (Singular Hours) Lublin 1966.

Filler, Witold: *Teatr, jaki jest* (The Theatre as It Is). Cracow 1967.

Greń, Zygmunt: *Godzina przestrogi* (The Hour of Warning). Cracow 1964.

Greń, Zygmunt: *Teatr i absurdy* (The Theatre and Absurdities) Warsaw 1967.

Greń, Zygmunt: *Wejście na scenę* (Stage Entrance). Poznań 1968.

Kott, Jan: *Jak się wam podoba* (As You Like It). Warsaw 1955.

Kott, Jan: *Poskromienie złośników* (Taming of the Shrews) Warsaw 1957.

Kott, Jan: *Miarka za miarkę* (Measure for Measure). Warsaw 1962.

Karczewska, Wanda: *Dzień powszedni teatru* (The Theatre's Common Day) Łódź 1970.

Kelera, Józef: *Kpiarze i moraliści* (Mockers and Moralists). Cracow 1966.

Kelera, Józef: *Pojedynki o teatr* (Duels for the Theatre) Wrocław 1969.

Kubacki, Wacław: *Na scenie* (On the Stage). Warsaw 1962.

Kubacki, Wacław: *W wyobraźni* (In the Imagination). Warsaw 1964.

Kreczmar, Jerzy: *Polemiki teatralne* (Theatre Polemic). Warsaw 1956.

Natanson, Wojciech: *Szkice teatralne* (Theatre Sketches). Cracow 1955.

Natanson, Wojciech: *Do trzech razy sztuka* (Three Strikes and You're Out). Cracow 1958.

Natanson, Wojciech: *Godzina teatru* (An Hour of the Theatre). Warsaw 1962.

Natanson, Wojciech: *Godzina dramatu* (An Hour of the Drama). Poznań 1970.

Pomianowski, Jerzy: *Z widowni* (From the Auditorium). Warsaw 1953.

Pomianowski, Jerzy: *Więcej kurażu* (More Courage). Warsaw 1956.

Pomianowski, Jerzy: *Sezon w czyśćcu* (A Season in Purgatory). Warsaw 1960.

Puzyna, Konstanty: *To co teatralne* (What is Theatrical) Warsaw 1960.

Vogler, Henryk: *Przygody w teatrze* (Adventures in the Theatre) Cracow 1960.

Wiech: *Ksiuty z Melpomeną* (Spooning with Melpomene) Warsaw 1963.

Wirth, Andrzej: *Siedem prób* (Seven Rehearsals). Warsaw 1962.

Wirth, Andrzej: *Teatr, jaki mógłby być* (The Theatre as It Could Be). Warsaw 1964.

Wojdowski, Bogdan: *Próba bez kostiumu* (Rehearsal without a Costume). Warsaw 1966.

Wolicki, Krzysztof: *Wszystko jedno co o 19.30* (No Matter What at 7:30 p. m.) Warsaw 1969.

Hausbrandt, Andrzej: *Teatr...? Rozmyślania w antraktach* (The Theatre? Reflections During Intermissions) Warsaw 1970.

Hausbrandt, Andrzej: Polish Theatrical Audiences in Figures. Warsaw 1970.